COOKING WITH WINE

By the Editors of *Sunset Books* and *Sunset Magazine*

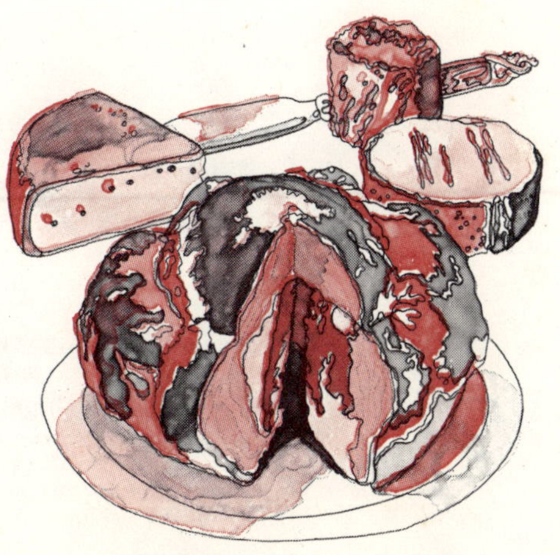

LANE BOOKS • MENLO PARK, CALIFORNIA

Edited by Judith A. Gaulke

Special Consultant: Jerry Anne DiVecchio
ASSOCIATE HOME ECONOMICS EDITOR,
SUNSET MAGAZINE

Design: Lawrence A. Laukhuf

Illustrations: Alyson Smith Gonsalves

Cover: Boeuf Bourguignonne, page 30
Photographed by George Selland, Moss Photography
Design Consultant: John Flack

Executive Editor, Sunset Books: David E. Clark
Third Printing April 1973

Library of Congress No. 78-180524. Title No. 376-02931-5.
Lithographed in the United States.

Contents

INTRODUCTION TO WINE

There is really nothing mysterious about cooking with wine. It may seem an adventurous ingredient, but it is as basic to good cooking as salt, garlic, or lemon juice. If you enjoy good eating, wine belongs in your kitchen.

There is ample tradition (or habit) to back such a stand. Multitudes of great dishes have pleased generations of tastes; consider the classic boeuf à la bourguignonne, a French version of beef stew from Burgundy; or fondue from Switzerland, a cheese melted in white wine.

Cooking with wine is a much older practice in European countries than in America. But American cooks are always borrowing food traditions from other countries. The combination of new awareness and an increased availability of wine in the United States in recent years has encouraged more and more cooks to discover wine as a cooking ingredient.

In European kitchens the wine used, more than likely, will be a local wine (or whatever is on hand) from that district. Here the choice is much wider. It is possible to use the wines of foreign countries or those produced in the states with equally good results.

A confident cook may add wine at her own whim, but most of us feel more assured if we have specific instructions to follow for the type and amount of wine to use. Here we have compiled a guide blending food and wine beneficial to both the experienced cook and the novice.

Each recipe was selected because wine favorably influenced the final results; subtly, when a few spoonfuls of Sherry are stirred into a tureen of soup; robustly, when a whole bottle of hearty red wine becomes the foundation of a beef marinade. All recipes were thoroughly tested in the test kitchens of Sunset Magazine and were chosen to give variety to the wonderful ways wine can be used in cooking.

WHY USE WINE

Good flavor and aroma—these are the principle things wine adds in cooking. Their combination can change a meal from plain to fancy. (The ordinary hamburger becomes downright impressive when cooked in red wine.) Along with flavor and aroma, wine also contributes nutritional value—notably minerals, sugar, and some vitamins. Mild acids in wine (malic and tartaric) have a tenderizing effect on meat through lengthy marinating or long slow simmering.

What influence does the alcohol have in wine cookery? When heated to 172.4° alcohol converts to vapor. This is long before water boils at 212°. When any dish comes to boiling, be assured that the alcohol has evaporated leaving behind only the delightful wine flavor and aroma. (Note that the directions for warm wine punches caution against overheating, to preserve the alcohol.)

CHOOSING AND USING WINE

Choosing can be confusing—at least at first. But choosing wine can be half the fun. Any wine that tastes good to you will have qualities you want for cooking. Discover some of the choices you can make by using the Wine Charts on pages 8 and 9. These capsule-size wine cooking lessons categorize wines according to color, name, and general flavor description.

What wines in what foods—this is a question with no pat answer as there is no universal rule to cover all cooking situations (it would take some of the fun out of experimenting if there were). The wine you plan to drink with dinner can be a good one to use in preparation of the entrée. Wine can be used as a seasoning for almost any dish in almost any course. And you can use wine in almost any cooking method—marinating, basting, baking, saucing, deglazing, or dressing a salad.

For the cook's convenience, this book is divided into chapters that relate to menu planning: appetizers, soups, salads, entrées, vegetables, desserts, and blended beverages. For each, directions are given for adding wine at a specific time for a particular purpose.

We have provided a wine cookery chart on page 78 to help you narrow your choices. This chart indicates wine types that are most acceptable and complementary for different food categories. If, for instance, you would like to add wine to a chicken gravy to perk it up a bit, check the chart to see which wines are suggested. It will list wines to enhance the flavor of that particular gravy and tell how much you should add for each serving. (As with most seasonings, when in doubt, too little is preferable to too much.)

When to add wine: If the fresh flavor of the wine itself is to predominate, add it just before serving the dish you are preparing. This will give it that distinctive finishing touch. If wine is used to accent and blend other food flavors, to tenderize, or to marinate, add it in the beginning of the preparation. Many recipes call for a wine addition at both the beginning and the end.

WINE TERMINOLOGY

Now for some terms. The wine language used in this book is intimate with the wines of California, but the general information pertains to all wines. (For example, when we say a wine is *dry*, we mean there is an absence of sweetness.)

Table Wine

Table wines can be red, white, or pink. All contain 13% alcohol or less and are generally served with meals. Let us first discover the two major wine classifications in California—*generic* and *varietal*.

What is a Generic Wine: Most generic wines are named for districts in Europe which produce wine having similar characteristics such as Burgundy or Chianti. Other generic wines are named for their color, such as Claret or Rosé. Several grape varieties are usually present in each wine but none dominates. Vintners have different notions as to how their generic wines should taste, hence one may find a notable difference between the same kind of generic wine from one vintner to the next.

Characteristically, generic wines are less expensive than varietal wines. Dry jug wines are predominantly generics and make good, practical choices for cooking.

What is a Varietal Wine: Varietal wines are named for the grapes from which they are made. California law requires a varietal wine to contain 51% (though it may contain 100%) of the grape variety for which it is named. It should also have the distinctive color, aroma, and flavor of the particular grape. Examples are Cabernet Sauvignon, Barbera, Chardonnay, and Sylvaner.

Proprietary wine: Sometimes a winemaker comes up with a wine blend that is unique to his winery and does not conform to the varietal or generic classes. These are known as proprietary wines and carry coined or descriptive names. Examples are Rubion, Vino da Tavola, Barenblut.

Sparkling wine: Champagne and sparkling wines fall into a category all their own. A second fermentation is induced in young wine to produce the bubbles. (Wines that have mechanically induced bubbles are labeled Carbonated Wine.) They range in flavor from dry to sweet and contain 12% alcohol. Sparkling wines are almost never called for in cooking per se, but they can add a most festive touch to punch drinks or when poured over fresh fruit. Sparkling wine types include Champagne, Crackling Rosé, Sparkling Burgundy, Cold Duck.

Appetizers and Dessert Wines

These wines are preserved in part by a greater percentage of alcohol (17 to 20%) so they can be recorked and stored for a period without spoiling. Appetizer and dessert wines range from very sweet to very dry. The drier varieties are traditionally served before the meal, where the sweeter ones are preferred after.

Because they are less perishable, dry Vermouth and a dry or medium Sherry are extremely popular with the cook; Sherry is possibly the most versatile wine in cooking, as it has an affinity for almost all foods with its rich nutty flavor. Dry Vermouth can be used in place of a dry white wine when the quantity is not excessive.

Fruit wines. These are produced by fermentation from fruit other than grapes. Most of them range from 12 to 20% in alcohol content. Typical examples are those made from berries, apples, apricots, peaches, pears, and cherries. Many have remarkable fresh fruit flavor.

Flavored wines. When a wine is flavored with natural, not chemical or artificial ingredients, such as fruit juice, coffee, or herbs, then it is called a flavored wine. Most tend to be sweet and have an alcoholic content ranging from 12 to 20%. (Because Vermouth is also an herb-flavored wine, it technically belongs in this category.) Flavored wines usually have proprietary names such as Spañada, Key Largo, Tyrolia, and Tangor.

Cooking wine. A wine that is labeled Cooking Wine has been salted according to government specifications, and for most tastes, it is rendered unpalatable as a beverage. The recipes in this book were tested with beverage wines, not cooking wine; if you substitute with a cooking wine you must reduce the salt, adjusting the seasoning to taste.

A SUGGESTED WINE "STARTER SET"

Instead of having to dash off to the store whenever you want to use some wine in cooking, it is easier to maintain a small stock of wines on hand to use when needed. Just one bottle of wine in the kitchen affords many cooking opportunities, but as your taste becomes more curious, your wine kitchen can become as sophisticated as your purse dictates. You may already have favorites, but if not, this is an adequate, flexible starter stock.

- 1 bottle of generic red wine (such as Burgundy)
- 1 bottle of generic white wine (such as Chablis)
- 1 bottle dry or medium Sherry
- 1 bottle dry Vermouth
- 1 bottle of a sweet dessert wine (such as Ruby Port)
- 1 bottle of brandy (distilled from wine) a luxurious addition . . . especially if you enjoy the idea of flaming desserts.

If these wines are to be used for cooking purposes only, you might want to buy them in convenient half-bottle sizes.

HOW OFTEN TO USE WINE

It is probably good advice not to use wine in every dish in the same menu. It would have a very repetitious, tiresome effect so that nothing tastes "special". The same would be true if you served lemon chicken accompanied by lemon salad dressing and lemon chiffon pie all in one dinner or put a lot of the same herbs in all dishes served. A restrained touch is a sound approach.

ONCE OPENED, WHAT THEN

As soon as a dry wine (which contains about 12% alcohol) is opened and exposed to the air it becomes subject to spoilage. In a week or less the wine flavor may begin to change. Any wine not consumed at a meal or used up in one cooking session should be tightly recorked and refrigerated. Most table wines will keep a few days (up to a week) if so treated. Decanting into smaller containers will lessen the amount of air the wine is exposed to and minimize the chance of it becoming vinegary. If the opened wine is to be used *only* for cooking, the little trick of adding a few drops of salad oil to film over the top surface will keep it sound even longer. Oil, when added in such an insignificant amount, will not hurt most dishes.

Appetizer and dessert wines, with their higher alcohol content, will last months if recorked tightly and kept in a cool, dark place.

SOME INNOVATIVE TIPS

Using the wine cookery chart on page 78 as a guide you might start with these general proposals:

- Use wine in place of part of the liquid in preparing dry sauce mixes, such as spaghetti.
- After sautéing meat, pour a few tablespoons of wine into the same pan and combine it with any browned particles left from the meat. Pour this combination over the meat.
- Use wine, to taste, as part of the liquid in cakes, batters, cooky doughs, puddings, or pie fillings.
- Use as part of the liquid, to suit your taste, in preparing a favorite soup, frozen soup, or soup from a mix. Or add a spoonful or two of wine to a serving of soup.
- In stews, replace part of the liquid with wine; use more the next time if you feel you would like the flavor.
- Stir a little wine to taste into homemade gravy, or gravy made by a shortcut method.
- Using wine as part of the measured liquid add, to taste, when preparing gelatin desserts or salads.
- Add, to taste, when reheating leftover meat, fish, or poultry dishes, or converting them to second meal entrées.
- Choose complementary wines to douse fresh, frozen, or canned fruits.
- Frozen vegetables with cream sauce are nicely accented by the addition of a tablespoon or two of white wine.
- Jellies can use part wine as a substitute for fruit juice in recipes that include pectin.

HOW ABOUT SERVING WINE WITH FOODS

Consider the wine you drink as a friend of the food . . . you can relax and enjoy one you've known awhile or branch out and meet one that is new and interesting. If you like it, it's right.

This book sticks to making general suggestions for cooking with wine. There are no suggestions for choosing wines to be served with foods, but in many instances the wine called for in the recipe will complement the dish as a beverage. If you have no preference it might be well to refer to the old adage claiming "red wines with red meats; white wines with white meats." Often the back labels on wine bottles contain helpful information to aid you in narrowing your selection.

AIDS FOR RECIPE READING

1. Each recipe in this book suggests in its introduction 2 wines we think go particularly well with that dish. For example it might read: Use a wine such as dry Sauterne (generic) or Sauvignon Blanc (varietal).
2. In the ingredient list for each recipe the kind of wine called for will be listed in **BOLD** type. For example: **white wine**. Just by scanning the ingredient list you can tell if you have it on hand or not. If you do not have the specific wine called for in a recipe introduction, refer to the wine charts on page 8 or 9 for a comparable wine. Feel free to use your own choice of wines—the ones given are only suggestions.

Oven Rump Roast

Use a wine such as a Burgundy or a Gamay

- 6-pound boneless rump roast
- 2 tablespoons salt
- 1 teaspoon dry mustard
- ¼ teaspoon *each* garlic salt and pepper
- Unseasoned meat tenderizer (optional)
- 1 tablespoon catsup
- 1 teaspoon Worcestershire
- ½ cup **dry red wine**

Rub the roast with salt, mustard, garlic salt, and pepper. (Use meat tenderizer as directed on package, if desired.) Insert meat thermometer into center of thickest part of roast, and place on a rack in a shallow baking pan.

Mix together catsup, Worcestershire, and wine; brush meat with this basting sauce. Roast in a 325° oven about 1 hour and 45 minutes or until meat thermometer registers 130° for rare (cook 18 minutes per pound). Baste with wine sauce several times during roasting; use all the sauce.

Let meat stand at room temperature 10 minutes to set juices, then slice and serve. Skim pan drippings of fat and serve with meat. Makes 10 servings.

These are some specific red wine choices you might want to consider using in this recipe: Burgundy (generic) or Gamay (varietal).

Heavy black print makes it easy to see the general wine required: **dry red wine.**

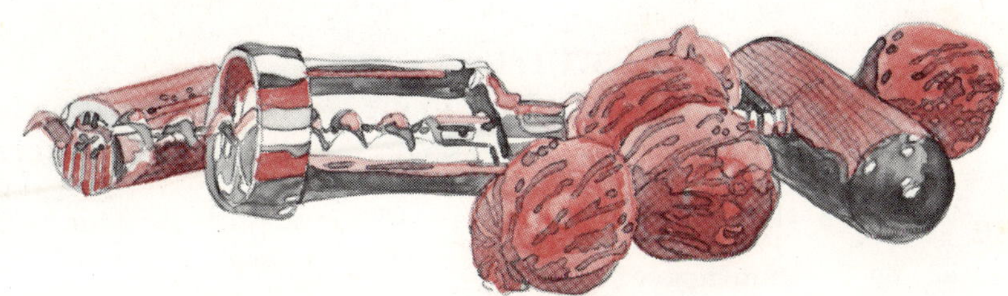

WINE CHART

GENERIC TABLE WINES

Wines of similar characteristics; some originally named for the European district from which they came.

WHITE

Light to medium dry wines

Rhine wine
White Chianti

Full flavored, dry, sometimes fruity

Chablis
Dry Sauterne
Mountain White

Medium-sweet, to quite sweet

Haut Sauterne
Light Muscat
Sweet Sauterne
"Chateau" White wines

ROSÉ

Light and fruity, usually medium-dry

Vin Rosé Rosé

RED

Dry, often pleasantly tart, medium to full bodied

Burgundy
Chianti
Claret
Mountain Red

Mellow, medium body, hearty flavor with a touch of sweetness

Barberone
Vino Rosso

VARIETAL TABLE WINES

Named for grapes from which they are made.

WHITE

Light, crisp, pleasantly dry

Emerald Riesling*
Gewürztraminer*
Green Hungarian*
Grey Riesling
Johannisberg (or White) Riesling
Sylvaner
Traminer
Riesling

Rich, full flavor, usually dry

Chardonnay (Pinot Chardonnay)
Chenin Blanc (White Pinot)*
Dry Semillon
Pinot Blanc
Sauvignon Blanc

Medium to pronounced sweetness

Malvasia Bianca
Muscat Bordelaise
Muscat Canelli
Sweet Semillon

*May tend to have sweetness

ROSÉ

Light, fruity, dry to slightly sweet

Cabernet Rosé
Gamay Rosé
Grenache Rosé
Grignolino Rosé
Zinfandel Rosé

RED

Fresh, fruity, dry, aromatic, light to medium body

- Cabernet
- Gamay
- Gamay Beaujolais
- Grignolino
- Pinot St. George (Red Pinot)
- Ruby Cabernet
- Zinfandel

Rich, red wines, distinct flavor, medium to full body.

- Barbera
- Cabernet Sauvignon
- Charbono
- Petite Sirah
- Pinot Noir

SPARKLING WINES

CHAMPAGNE

White, effervescent wines

- Natural—very dry
- Brut—dry
- Extra Dry—touch of sweetness
- Dry—medium sweet
- Sec—sweet
- Demi-Sec—very sweet

ROSÉ

Medium dry to sweet

- Pink Champagne
- Crackling Rosé

RED

Slightly sweet, full flavored

- Sparkling Burgundy
- Cold Duck (blend of Burgundy and Champagne)

MUSCAT

Sweet, Muscat flavor

Sparkling Muscat   Moscato Spumante   Moscato Amabile

Carbonated: Table wines which have mechanically induced bubbles.

APPETIZER AND DESSERT WINES

SHERRY

Flavor range from light to full, very dry to sweet

- Cocktail
- Medium dry
- Dry
- Cream

VERMOUTH

Herbal flavor dry is white, sweet is dark red, half and half is a blend of these two

Dry   Half and Half   Sweet

PORT

Name denotes color, full flavored, sweet

Ruby   Tawny   Tinta   White

MUSCATEL

Sweet, carry distinct flavor of the muscat grape

Black Muscat   Muscatel (gold or red)
Muscat Frontignan

OTHERS

- Angelica—sweet
- Madeira—may be dry to sweet
- Tokay—sweet
- Marsala—dry to sweet
- Sweet white wines (see page 8)

UNCORKING THE APPETITE

Appetizer and First Course Delights

A touch of wine adds a subtle, enjoyable sophistication to these appetizers and first-course dishes. All appetizers are designed to be finger food—pâtés and cheese mixtures to spread, dips for crunchy tidbits or fruit. For an extended entertaining hour there are chafing dish specialties and skewered hot appetizers.

The first courses are all sit down or eat-off-a-plate kind. Coquilles St. Jacques to pasta—all are meant to delight the palate.

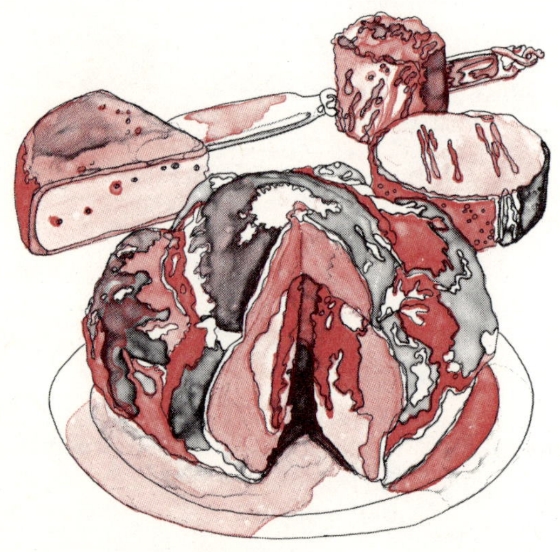

Sherried Shrimp with Tangy Sauce

Shrimp marinated several hours in Sherry take on a rich nutty flavor when cooked; serve with a piquant sauce.

- 1½ pounds raw shrimp or prawns
- ½ cup **dry Sherry**
- 4 tablespoons (⅛ lb.) butter
- ½ teaspoon garlic salt
- ¼ cup grated Parmesan cheese
- Tangy sauce (recipe follows)

Peel and devein shrimp. Place in a bowl and pour Sherry over them. Let marinate for several hours in a refrigerator. Melt butter in frying pan over low heat. Add shrimp and Sherry. Sprinkle with garlic salt and simmer for 10 to 15 minutes or until shrimp are bright pink and firm. Just before serving, sprinkle cheese over shrimp, and place under broiler just until cheese is lightly browned. Serve hot with toothpicks to dip shrimp into tangy sauce. Makes appetizers for 6 to 8 people.

Tangy Sauce:

- ½ cup mayonnaise
- 2 teaspoons lemon juice
- 1 tablespoon catsup
- 2 teaspoons *each* Worcestershire and prepared mustard

Thoroughly mix mayonnaise, lemon juice, catsup, Worcestershire, and mustard; chill until ready to use. Makes about ½ cup sauce.

Pork Balls in Cheese Dip

Use a wine such as a Chablis or a Pinot Blanc in this appetizer dip.

- 2 ounces imported Liederkranz or Camembert cheese
- 2 tablespoons butter or margarine
- ¼ cup coarsely chopped onion
- 1 pound boneless fully-cooked ham, ground
- ½ pound boneless lean pork, ground
- ⅓ cup *each* milk and fine dry bread crumbs
- 2 eggs
- 2 tablespoons all-purpose flour
- ¾ cup water
- ½ cup **dry white wine**
- 1 teaspoon chicken stock base or 1 chicken bouillon cube

Cut off the outside rind of the cheese and discard; set cheese aside. In a small saucepan over medium-high heat melt the butter; add the onion and sauté until golden, about 4 minutes. Remove from heat and, with a slotted spoon, transfer onions to a bowl; reserve butter in pan. Add to the onions the ham, pork, milk, bread crumbs, and eggs. Mix together with your fingers until blended. Shape into 1-inch balls and set about 1 inch apart on greased rimmed baking sheets. Bake in a 500° oven, turning as needed to brown well on all sides, about 7 to 10 minutes. Spoon into a small serving bowl and keep warm while you make sauce.

Stir the flour into reserved butter; stir over medium-high heat until bubbly. Remove from heat and gradually stir in water and wine. Add chicken stock base and cook, stirring, until the mixture boils and thickens; remove from heat. Add cheese and stir until it melts. Pour into a serving bowl. Keep sauce and meatballs warm on an electric warming tray or in chafing dishes with hot water jackets. Spear meatballs with toothpicks to dip into sauce. Makes enough sauce for 6 dozen meatballs.

Shrimp Appetizer Spread

- 1 large package (8 oz.) cream cheese (at room temperature)
- 3 tablespoons **dry Sherry**
- 1 clove garlic, mashed
- 1 green onion (white part only), finely minced
- 1½ teaspoons curry powder
- ¼ cup milk
- 1 cup (6 oz.) small cooked shrimp, or 1 can (4½ oz.) shrimp, drained
- Plain or onion-flavored crackers
- Raw vegetables such as carrot sticks, cauliflower buds, zucchini slices

Mix the cream cheese and Sherry together until smoothly blended. Stir in the garlic, onion, curry powder, and milk, then lightly mix in the shrimp until evenly distributed. Cover and refrigerate at least 3 hours or overnight to blend flavors.

Allow shrimp mixture to stand at room temperature for about 30 minutes to soften before serving. Arrange crackers or vegetables around the bowl of spread. Makes about 1½ cups.

(For fewer calories, omit cream cheese and milk replacing them with 1 pint cottage cheese, whirled smooth in a blender with the Sherry. Makes 2½ cups.)

Nippy Cheese Spread for Vegetables

Fresh raw vegetables spread or dipped into these cheese mixtures make relatively light before-dinner appetizers for those concerned with calories.

- 1½ cups shredded sharp Cheddar cheese
- ½ cup small curd cottage cheese
- ¼ cup (2 oz.) blue-veined cheese
- 3 tablespoons **dry Sherry**
- ¼ teaspoon Worcestershire
- 2 tablespoons chopped chives (fresh, frozen, or freeze-dried)
- Fresh raw vegetables such as carrot sticks, celery sticks, turnip slices, mushrooms, and cherry tomatoes

With an electric mixer or rotary beater, beat together the cheddar, cottage and blue-veined cheeses, Sherry, Worcestershire, and chives until well blended. Place in a small bowl. Serve alongside an assortment of raw vegetables; spread cheese on vegetables or dip vegetables into cheese. Makes 1½ cups spread.

Pears and Apples with Smoked Cheese Dip

Fresh fruit dipped in this smoked cheese and wine sauce makes a most refreshing variation on cheese fondue for an appetizer. Use a wine such as a dry Sauterne or a Sauvignon Blanc.

- 2 tablespoons butter
- 2 tablespoons all-purpose flour
- ½ teaspoon dry mustard
- 2 cups milk or half-and-half
- 3 cups (¾ lb.) shredded hickory-smoked process cheese
- ½ cup **dry white wine**
- 1 tablespoon **brandy** or **cognac**
- Large Bartlett pears and Jonathan apples (about 4 *each*)
- French bread chunks (optional)

Melt butter in a saucepan and blend in flour and mustard. Gradually add milk, stirring, and cook until thickened. Add cheese and stir until melted. Blend in wine and brandy.

Place cheese mixture in an attractive pan over a small candle warmer or in a fondue pot over its own heat source. Dip cored wedges of pears or apples and chunks of bread into sauce. Stir sauce occasionally; thin, if necessary, with more milk or half-and-half. Makes about 4 cups sauce or 8 to 10 servings.

Chicken Liver-Mushroom Pâté

Serving a subtly flavored, smooth pâté adds a certain sophistication to any party. Happily, this pâté is also easily prepared. Use a wine such as a dry Sauterne or a dry Semillon.

- ½ pound mushrooms
- 1 pound chicken livers
- 1 teaspoon *each* garlic salt and paprika
- ⅓ cup finely chopped green onion, including part of tops
- ¾ cup (⅜ lb.) butter
- ⅓ cup **dry white wine**
- ¼ teaspoon dill weed
- 3 drops liquid hot pepper seasoning
- Salt
- Plain or Sesame crackers

In a medium-sized frying pan over medium-high heat simmer the mushrooms, chicken livers, garlic salt, paprika, and onion in ¼ cup of the butter for 5 minutes. Add wine, dill weed, and liquid hot pepper seasoning. Cover and simmer slowly 5 to 10 minutes more or until livers are just firm.

Cool slightly and whirl smooth in a blender. Blend in the remaining ½ cup butter and add salt to taste. Chill thoroughly. Serve to spread on crackers. Makes 3 cups.

Sherried Camembert with Grapes

Here the small addition of Sherry alters the cheese sufficiently to give it an intriguing new character.

- 1 whole (about 4½ oz.) ripe Danish Camembert cheese
- 2 tablespoons **cream Sherry** or **dry Sherry**
- ¼ cup chopped walnuts
- Fresh grapes
- Unsalted wheat crackers

Cut the rind from the Camembert and discard. Mash cheese with the Sherry until smoothly blended. Reshape cheese as it was originally. Coat top with walnuts. Chill to firm. When ready to serve, let stand at room temperature for 20 minutes; serve with grapes and unsalted wheat crackers. Makes 4 servings.

Appetizer Meatballs in Spicy Sauce

Baking meatballs at high heat is an easy way to cook them in large quantities. They can be completely prepared a day in advance. A hearty red wine goes well in the sauce. Use a wine such as a Burgundy or a Zinfandel.

- ⅓ cup firmly packed brown sugar
- 1 can (8 oz.) tomato sauce
- 3 tablespoons lemon juice
- ⅛ teaspoon garlic salt
- ½ cup **dry red wine**
- 1 small potato, peeled
- 1 pound lean ground beef
- 1 small onion, finely minced
- 1 egg
- 1 teaspoon salt

In a saucepan, combine the brown sugar, tomato sauce, lemon juice, garlic salt, and wine. Bring to boiling, stirring; reduce heat, and allow to simmer gently, uncovered, until sauce is thickened, about 20 minutes.

Finely shred enough potato to make ⅓ cup. Combine potato with meat, onion, egg, and salt until blended; shape into balls the size of large marbles.

Arrange meatballs on a shallow baking pan. Put into a 500° oven for 4 to 5 minutes, or until lightly browned. Remove and add to the prepared sauce, including any pan juices. Cool, then cover and refrigerate if made ahead.

To serve, heat meatballs and sauce together slowly and serve hot. Spear with toothpicks. Makes about 5 dozen meatballs.

Melon Platter with Chutney Dip

- 2 large packages (8 oz. *each*) cream cheese
- ¼ cup **dry Sherry**
- 1 teaspoon seasoned salt
- ½ teaspoon curry powder
- ⅓ cup chopped Major Grey's chutney
- 2 tablespoons finely chopped green onion, including part of the tops
- ½ to 1 cup sour cream
- Assorted melon balls and cubes (cantaloupe, watermelon, Crenshaw melon, and honeydew)

Beat cream cheese smooth with Sherry, seasoned salt, and curry powder. Stir in chutney, green onion, and sour cream. Pour into a serving bowl. Chill.

To serve, arrange chilled melon balls and cubes in groups on a large platter along with chutney dip and cocktail picks to spear the fruit for dipping. Makes about 2½ cups dip.

Chutney Peanut Butter Canapés

Have your bakery slice loaves of an egg bread or a good rye lengthwise making large slices to speed the assembly of these canapés. Use a wine such as a Burgundy or a Gamay Beaujolais.

- ¾ cup chunk-style peanut butter
- 1 small package (3 oz.) cream cheese
- ¼ teaspoon seasoned salt
- ¼ cup **dry red wine**
- ¼ teaspoon Worcestershire
- 1½ cups Major Grey's chutney, finely chopped
- Toasted, buttered egg or rye bread slices, crusts removed

Blend well the peanut butter, cream cheese, salt, wine, Worcestershire, and chutney. Spread on toast. Cut into individual triangles or fingers. Makes 2 cups spread.

Easy Mushrooms Bourguignonne

Bourguignonne refers to the Burgundy region of France and usually means the dish, like these mushrooms, is cooked with a Burgundy-style wine. Use a wine such as a Burgundy or a Gamay.

- 1 pound medium-sized fresh mushrooms
- 1 cup **dry red wine**
- 1 tablespoon *each* minced shallots (or green onions) and minced parsley
- 1 clove garlic, crushed
- ¼ cup (⅛ lb.) butter
- ¼ teaspoon salt
- Black pepper to taste

Wash mushrooms and remove stems (reserve for future use). Put caps in a frying pan with wine, shallots, parsley, garlic, butter, salt, and pepper. Simmer uncovered for 6 to 7 minutes, stirring. Discard garlic. Spear hot mushrooms with small wooden skewers. Makes about 3 dozen appetizers.

Turkey and Grapes in Patty Shells

Serve this attractive dish as the first course for an elegant dinner; or make it the light entrée for a brunch or lunch. Use a wine such as a Rhine, a Sylvaner, or a Grey Riesling.

- 1 package (10 oz.) frozen puff paste patty shells or baked patty shells from a bakery
- 1 can (10¼ oz.) white sauce
- 2 tablespoons **dry white wine**
- About 1½ cups diced cooked turkey or 2 cans (5 oz. *each*) boned turkey meat
- ⅛ teaspoon rosemary
- About 1½ cups stemmed seedless grapes, or 1 can (1 lb.) seedless grapes, drained
- Salt to taste
- Sliced toasted almonds for garnish

Bake the frozen patty shells according to directions on the box or warm the bakery shells in a 350° oven for about 10 minutes. Meanwhile, in a saucepan over medium-high heat, bring to simmering the white sauce, wine, turkey, and rosemary. Stir in grapes and add salt to taste. Spoon into warm patty shells and top each serving with almonds. Makes 6 servings.

Turkey Crêpes

Here's another impressive way to present leftover turkey: Blend meat with a rich cream-wine sauce, wrap it in tender crêpes, top with avocados, and serve as a first course or light brunch entrée. Use a wine such as a Chablis or a Chenin Blanc.

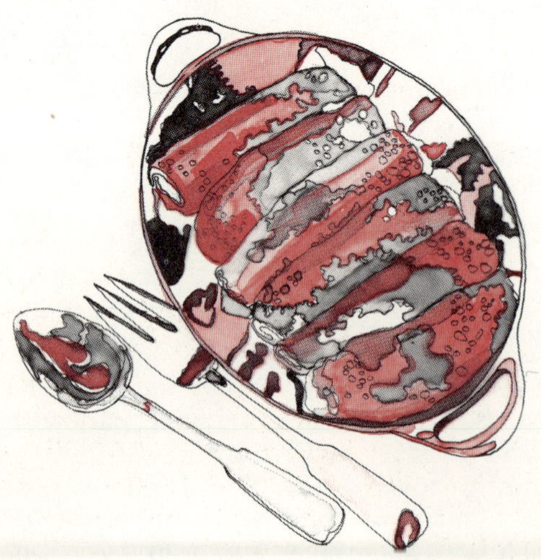

- 5 tablespoons *each* butter and all-purpose flour
- 1 teaspoon salt
- ⅛ teaspoon pepper
- 1 cup *each* milk and regular-strength chicken broth (or broth made from turkey carcass)
- ½ teaspoon Worcestershire
- 2 tablespoons minced parsley
- 1 cup shredded Swiss cheese
- ¾ cup **dry white wine**
- 2 cups diced cooked turkey
- ½ cup chopped ripe olives
- 1 ripe avocado, peeled, pitted, and sliced
- 12 crêpes, 7 or 8 inches in diameter (recipe follows)
- Paprika

In a saucepan melt butter and blend with flour, salt, and pepper. Gradually blend in milk, broth, and Worcestershire. Cook, stirring, until thickened. Stir in parsley, ¾ cup of the cheese, and the wine. Keep sauce warm; measure out 1 cup and combine with turkey and olives. Divide the mixture evenly among crêpes placing on uncooked side. Fold crêpes over filling. Arrange in a single layer in a baking dish. Arrange avocado on top. Cover with reserved sauce. Sprinkle with remaining cheese, and paprika.

Bake in a 375° oven for 10 minutes, then broil quickly until top is lightly browned. Makes 6 servings.

Crêpes:

- 2 eggs
- 1 cup milk
- ¾ cup all-purpose flour
- ⅛ teaspoon salt

Beat together until smooth the eggs, milk, flour, and salt. Pour about 2 tablespoons of batter in a buttered 7 or 8-inch frying pan and cook over medium heat until surface is dry to touch. Invert onto a flat pan. Repeat until all batter is used. Use hot, or stack and chill if made ahead, but return to room temperature before separating crêpes or they will tear. Makes 12 crêpes.

Coquilles St. Jacques in Butter

This easy version of the classic French dish can be prepared ahead of time. Use a wine such as a Chablis or a Pinot Blanc.

1½ pounds scallops
1½ cups **dry white wine**
½ cup (¼ lb.) melted butter
2 tablespoons minced parsley
Paprika

Wash and drain scallops. Bring wine to a boil in a saucepan, add scallops, cover, and simmer for 8 to 10 minutes or until scallops are opaque through (cut one to test). Lift out scallops and cut in large slices (reserve broth for fish soups).

Arrange scallops in 4 scallop baking shells or individual casseroles. Spoon 2 tablespoons melted butter over top of each filled shell. Sprinkle 1½ teaspoons parsley over each, then sprinkle with paprika. To serve heat in a 350° oven for 5 minutes. Makes 4 servings.

Crab and Mushrooms Supreme on Muffins

3 tablespoons butter
¾ pound mushrooms, thinly sliced
Juice of ½ lemon (about 1½ tablespoons)
¼ cup **dry Sherry**
1 cup sour cream
¾ pound fresh crab meat or 2 cans (7½,oz. *each*) crab, drained
3 tablespoons grated Parmesan cheese
4 English muffins
1 tablespoon minced parsley for garnish

Melt 1 tablespoon of the butter in a large frying pan, add mushrooms, and sprinkle with the lemon juice; sauté until mushrooms are limp. Add Sherry and boil until liquid is reduced one half. Remove from heat and stir in sour cream, mixing until blended. Add crab meat and grated cheese and gently heat through; do not boil. Split and butter muffins with remaining butter; then toast muffins lightly. Arrange them on a serving platter or individual plates and spoon over crab sauce. Sprinkle with parsley. Makes 4 servings.

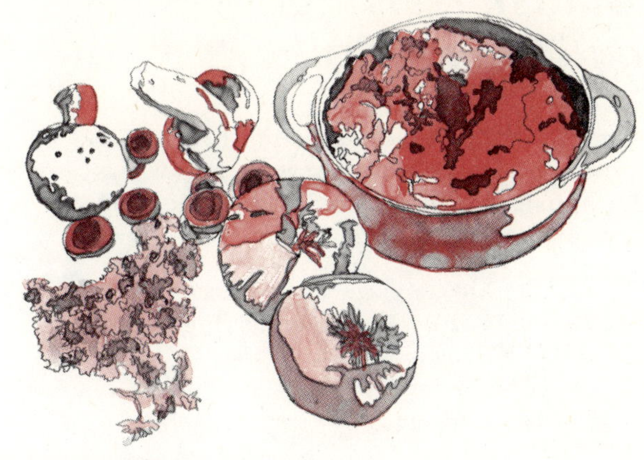

Roquefort Crisps

3 ounces Roquefort cheese
2 tablespoons *each* butter and **brandy**
3 large red apples
Lemon juice
Crackers

Mix cheese, butter, and brandy in a small bowl; cover and keep refrigerated overnight or until needed. Core apples and leave unpeeled. Cut into ½-inch slices and dip in lemon juice to prevent darkening. Spread the cheese-butter-brandy mixture on apples or crackers. Makes about ½ cup spread.

Stuffed Mushroom Caps

½ pound small mushrooms
About 2 tablespoons melted butter
4 tablespoons soft butter
1 small clove garlic, minced or mashed
3 tablespoons finely diced or shredded jack cheese
2 tablespoons **dry red wine**
1 teaspoon soy sauce
⅓ cup finely crushed cracker crumbs

Remove stems from mushrooms and save for other uses. Brush mushroom caps with the melted butter. Combine soft butter with garlic, add cheese, and mix in well. Add wine and soy sauce, then the cracker crumbs, blending to make a paste. Place on a rimmed baking sheet and broil about 5 inches from heat for about 3 minutes, or until bubbly and lightly browned. Spear with toothpicks to eat. Makes 3 to 4 servings.

Danish Herring and Caviar Rolls

Served with dark bread, this herring and caviar combination makes a very attractive first course. Lumpfish caviar is pleasing with herring, yet it is less expensive than most varieties.

- ⅔ cup **dry Sherry**
- 2 cans (5½ oz. *each*) matjes herring, drained
- 1 jar (2 oz.) lumpfish caviar
- 1 hard-cooked egg
- Parsley sprigs
- Sour cream
- Dark bread rounds

Pour Sherry into an 8-inch square baking pan. Place herring fillets in a single layer, skin side up in the Sherry, cover and refrigerate for 1 hour. Remove fillets from Sherry and slice each in half lengthwise. Spread each half with an equal amount of caviar, using all, and carefully roll pinwheel fashion.

Place rolled fillets on their side in a serving dish. Separately press white and yolk of egg through wire strainer, then sprinkle some of each over herring. Garnish with parsley. Pass sour cream to serve with herring. Serve with dark bread rounds. Eat with knife and fork. Makes 8 servings.

Mushroom-Stuffed Artichokes

Artichokes, trimmed down until only the inner bracts or leaves remain, are stuffed with a bacon and mushroom mixture. Use a wine such as a Rhine or a Sylvaner.

- 6 large artichokes (at least 3-inch diameter *each*)
- Boiling salted water
- 2 tablespoons *each* salad oil and lemon juice
- 6 slices bacon, diced
- 1 medium-sized onion, chopped
- ½ pound mushrooms, chopped
- 3 tablespoons chopped parsley
- 1 clove garlic, minced
- ½ cup tomato sauce
- ½ cup **dry white wine**
- 2 tablespoons butter

Cut off stem and top half of artichokes, discard. Pull off the outer bracts until you reach the pale yellow tender inner leaves. Trim base. Cook artichokes in a deep kettle, covered, in boiling salted water with the oil and lemon juice for 30 to 40 minutes, or until heart is tender when pierced. Drain upside down and let cool slightly. Spread outer leaves slightly and scrape out the center choke with a teaspoon.

While artichokes cook prepare stuffing. Cook bacon in a frying pan until crisp; remove from pan with slotted spoon and pour off half the drippings. Sauté onion and mushrooms in remaining drippings until limp. Add parsley, garlic, tomato sauce, ¼ cup of the wine, and cooked bacon; cover and simmer 10 minutes. Spoon stuffing into center of artichokes.

Arrange in baking pan with butter cut in small pieces, and remaining wine in the bottom. (You can refrigerate at this point.) Cover and bake in a 350° oven about 15 minutes (25 minutes if refrigerated), or until hot through. Serve on individual plates. Makes 6 servings.

Spinach Shrimp Tart

Shrimp, clams, spinach, mushrooms, and white wine blend harmoniously in this savory open-faced pie. Cut it in pie-shaped wedges and serve hot. Use a wine such as a Rhine or a Riesling.

- Pastry for a double crust 9-inch pie
- 1 can (7½ oz.) minced clams
- ½ cup whipping cream
- 2 tablespoons cornstarch
- 3 tablespoons **dry white wine**
- ⅛ teaspoon nutmeg
- 4 egg yolks
- ¼ cup shredded Parmesan cheese
- 2 packages (10 oz. *each*) frozen chopped spinach, thawed, and drained, or 1½ pounds fresh, well washed and drained spinach leaves, chopped
- ¼ pound cooked and shelled small shrimp
- ¼ pound mushrooms, sliced
- 2 tablespoons butter or margarine
- 1 clove garlic, minced

Prepare pastry shell using your own recipe or pie crust mix. Roll out all the dough and fit into a 10-inch pie pan, fluting edges for a single crust; or fit into a fluted 11-inch flan pan. Bake at 450° for 10 minutes.

Drain liquid from clams into a saucepan; add whipping cream and bring to a boil. Stir in a paste of cornstarch and wine; then, stirring, cook until thickened. Add nutmeg. Beat egg yolks; stir in the hot sauce and 3 tablespoons of the cheese. Mix in drained spinach, shrimp, and clams.

Sauté mushrooms in 1 tablespoon of the butter with garlic until limp; set aside 8 mushroom slices for garnish and add remainder to spinach mixture. Spread filling evenly in baked pastry shell and arrange reserved mushrooms on top. Sprinkle with remaining cheese. Melt remaining 1 tablespoon butter and drizzle over top. Bake at 350° for 20 to 25 minutes, or until set. Makes 8 to 10 servings.

Beef-Olive Spaghetti Sauce

A pasta course is traditionally served first in Italy; you might present this dish before a roast turkey or other large cut of meat. Use a wine such as a Chianti or a Barbera.

1½ pounds lean ground beef, crumbled
1 large onion, chopped
½ cup chopped green pepper
1 large clove garlic, minced or mashed
1 carrot, shredded
½ pound medium-sized mushrooms, quartered
2 tablespoons chopped parsley
1 can (1 lb.) whole tomatoes
1 can (8 oz.) tomato sauce
1 can (6 oz.) tomato paste
½ cup **dry red wine**
2 teaspoons spaghetti sauce seasoning (or 1 teaspoon basil, and ¼ teaspoon *each* savory, rosemary, and marjoram)
½ teaspoon *each* sugar and salt
⅛ teaspoon pepper
1 can (2¼ oz.) sliced ripe olives
Hot, cooked vermicelli, or fine spaghetti
Shredded Parmesan cheese

Brown beef well in a large frying pan. Reduce heat, add onion, green pepper, and garlic, and cook until onion is soft, stirring occasionally. Stir in carrot, mushrooms, parsley, whole tomatoes and liquid, tomato sauce, tomato paste, wine, spaghetti seasoning, sugar, salt, and pepper. Simmer, covered, for 1½ hours. Add olives and cook, uncovered, for about 30 minutes longer, until sauce reduced and thick. Serve hot spooned over hot spaghetti; pass cheese to sprinkle onto each portion according to taste. Makes 6 to 8 servings.

Sliced Steak Tartar

Thin slices of raw steak can stand in this flavorful marinade up to 3 days in the refrigerator. Have your meatman slice beef into uniform thin slices; or you can do it at home if the meat is frozen, then slightly thawed to slice. Use a wine such as a Burgundy or a Pinot Noir.

2 pound piece top round or sirloin steak, sliced ⅛ inch thick
1 cup finely chopped fresh parsley
Onion-red wine marinade (recipe follows)
4 to 5 mushrooms, sliced

Using a large bowl, alternate layers of meat slices and parsley. Pour hot marinade over meat. Cover and refrigerate from 1 to 3 days.

Remove from refrigerator about 20 minutes before serving. Arrange slices on a platter and spoon over a little marinade. Garnish with a few sliced raw mushrooms. Eat with knife and fork. Makes about 8 to 10 appetizer servings.

Onion-Red Wine Marinade:

1 cup chopped onions
¼ cup olive oil or salad oil
½ cup red wine vinegar
2 cloves garlic, minced
½ pound mushrooms, chopped
¾ cup **dry red wine**
2 teaspoons beef stock base
1 bay leaf
1 teaspoon crumbled oregano
¼ teaspoon *each* salt, pepper, and marjoram

In a large frying pan, sauté the onions in the oil until golden brown. Add the wine vinegar and garlic and cook down until liquid is reduced by half. Add the mushrooms, wine, beef stock base, bay leaf, oregano, salt, pepper, and marjoram; cover and simmer for 5 minutes.

SOUP AND SALAD SECRETS

Hot to Cold, Light to Hearty

Wine is a delightful flavoring element in hot or cold soups; it can cook with the ingredients to add subtlety, or it can be added at the last moment as a seasoning accent.

Chilled first-course soups are refreshing for a springtime brunch or a pleasant introduction to dinner.

Hot soups, predominantly light in substance with richly developed wine accents, are another delicious way to initiate a meal. If you like, taste the soup as you add wine, until the results are agreeable to you.

Instant Vichyssoise

This is a quick version of the well-known cold soup; it is made from frozen potato soup and needs no heating. Use a wine such as a Chablis or a White Pinot.

1 can (10¼ oz.) frozen potato soup
1 cup half-and-half
¼ cup **dry white wine**
Chopped hard-cooked egg

Whirl the soup and half-and-half in a blender until smooth, or force through a wire strainer. Add the wine and serve chilled. Garnish with chopped hard-cooked egg. Makes 2 or 3 servings.

Spiced Rhubarb Soup

This chilled, pale pink rhubarb soup makes a gracious introduction for warm weather luncheons. A light flowery wine complements the fruit. Use a wine such as a Rhine or an Emerald Riesling.

4 cups (about 1¼ lbs.) diced rhubarb
4 cups water
1 cup sugar
1 teaspoon grated orange peel
3-inch stick cinnamon
2 tablespoons arrowroot or cornstarch
½ cup water
½ teaspoon vanilla
Few drops red food coloring (optional)
Whole cloves
Thin orange slices
About ½ cup **dry white wine,** chilled

Place rhubarb in a 3-quart pan with the 4 cups water, sugar, orange peel, and cinnamon. Bring to a boil, reduce heat, and simmer for about 20 minutes. Blend arrowroot with the ½ cup water and stir the mixture into the rhubarb. Bring to a boil, then remove from heat. Add vanilla and red food coloring to tint a delicate pink; cool. Place in a serving bowl (glass, if available, to show off the color) and refrigerate until thoroughly chilled. Serve garnished with clove-studded orange slices. Add about 1 tablespoon wine to each serving. Makes 6 to 8 servings.

Iced Fresh Tomato Soup

The secret for best flavor in this soup is to use very ripe tomatoes and a full-flavored dry white wine such as a Chablis or a dry Sauterne.

4 pounds tomatoes, fully ripe
¼ teaspoon basil
2 tablespoons chopped onion
1 cup canned condensed chicken broth
2 teaspoons sugar
½ teaspoon salt
¼ teaspoon pepper
1 cup **dry white wine**
Tiny cooked shelled shrimp for garnish

Remove ends from tomatoes. Cut each tomato into eighths and force with basil and onion through a food mill (or whirl until fairly smooth in a blender). Put into a bowl. Add chicken broth, sugar, salt, pepper, and white wine and blend well. Chill thoroughly. Stir before serving. Garnish with a few shrimp on top each bowl of soup. Makes 6 to 8 servings.

Chilled Sour Cream Cucumber Soup

Cucumbers and wine make a refreshing prelude to a hearty entrée. Use a wine such as a Chablis or a Chardonnay.

2 cups milk
3 eggs, beaten
1 cup *each* sour cream and regular-strength chicken broth
½ cup **dry white wine**
1½ cups finely chopped peeled cucumber
2 tablespoons finely chopped green onion, including part of tops
1 tablespoon finely chopped pimiento
1 teaspoon salt
¼ teaspoon dill weed

Scald milk over direct heat in top of a double boiler. Gradually stir some of the hot milk into beaten eggs, then return all to pan. Cook, stirring, over scalding hot (not boiling) water until mixture coats a spoon; takes 15 to 20 minutes. Remove from heat and cool. Gradually blend soup smooth with sour cream. Blend in broth, wine, cucumber, green onion, pimiento, salt, and dill weed. Chill thoroughly before serving. Makes about 1½ quarts or 6 to 8 servings.

Wine Consommé

This consommé is versatile and can be served hot, cold, or jellied. Use a wine such as a Claret or a Cabernet Sauvignon.

4 cups regular-strength beef broth
1 cup **dry red wine**
1 teaspoon sugar
Dash lemon juice
Salt and pepper to taste
Thin lemon slices

In a saucepan heat beef broth to boiling point and add wine, sugar, and lemon juice. Add salt and pepper to taste. Serve hot in soup cups garnished with lemon slices. Chill to serve cold. Makes 6 servings, about ¾ cup each.

Jellied Wine Consommé:

Soften 2 envelopes unflavored gelatin in ½ cup cold water, then add to beef broth as it heats, following the recipe above. Chill until set, then stir with a fork to break into small pieces. Spoon into soup bowls or cups and garnish with lemon slices.

Peach Champagne Soup

You can serve a fruit soup at a festive brunch or as a dessert. The fruit mellows first in still wine, then you ladle up the soup at the table pouring frothy Champagne into each serving. Visual and taste sensations are both delightful. Use a wine such as Rhine wine or Chenin Blanc.

12 medium-sized ripe peaches
Scalding water
1 small bottle (⅘ qt.) or 1¾ cups **fruity white wine**
Sugar to taste, starting with 1 tablespoon
1 bottle (⅘ qt.) chilled **Sec** or **Extra Dry Champagne**

Dip each peach in scalding water to loosen skin, then peel and cut each fruit in half, removing pit. Put peaches in a deep bowl and pour in the still wine; there should be just enough to cover fruit.

Add sugar (just barely sweeten; amount varies with the fruit and wine). Cover and chill at least 2 hours.

To serve, ladle 2 peach halves into each serving bowl, and an equal amount of the wine marinade;

then pour in an equal amount of Champagne (using it all), and eat at once. Makes 12 servings.

To make 6 servings, use only 6 peaches, sugar to taste, the small bottle (⅘ qt.) still wine and a small bottle (⅘ qt.) of Champagne.

Norwegian Wine Soup

Typical of many Scandinavian soups, this one is slightly thickened. Serve it either at the beginning or end of your meal. In addition to Sherry, use a wine such as a Rhine or a Johannisberg Riesling.

- 3 cups water
- 3-inch stick cinnamon
- ½ tablespoon *each* grated lemon and lime peel
- ½ teaspoon nutmeg
- 4 tablespoons quick-cooking tapioca
- 3 egg yolks
- ¾ cup sugar
- ½ cup **medium Sherry**
- 1½ cups **dry white wine**
- Dash of salt

In a saucepan boil together water, cinnamon, lemon and lime peels, and nutmeg for 5 minutes. Strain to leave a clear liquid. Add tapioca, bring to a boil, and continue to simmer, stirring, until tapioca is clear, about 20 minutes.

Meanwhile, beat egg yolks and sugar together until foamy. Remove cooked soup from heat and gradually add hot mixture to the eggs and mix well. Stir in wines. Serve hot in bowls or mugs. Makes about 1½ quarts or 6 to 8 servings.

French Onion Soup

There are three secrets to making good onion soup: Sauté onions very slowly, until they take on a rich caramel color; use a richly flavored beef broth; and select well aged natural Swiss cheese for its full, mellow taste. Use a wine such as a dry Sauterne or a Chablis.

- 3 large onions, thinly sliced
- ¼ cup butter
- 2 teaspoons all-purpose flour
- 6 cups regular-strength beef broth (canned or homemade)
- ⅓ cup **dry white wine**
- Salt and pepper to taste
- 8 slices, *each* ½-inch thick, crusty French bread
- Garlic butter
- 1 cup shredded Swiss cheese

In saucepan sauté onion very slowly in butter for about 30 minutes, stirring frequently until a rich caramel color. Sprinkle onions with flour; allow flour to brown slightly. Slowly stir in beef broth, and simmer for 15 minutes. Stir in white wine. Season to taste with salt and pepper. Toast the French bread slices and spread them with garlic butter. To serve, place toast in heated soup tureen or soup bowls; ladle soup over the toast. Cover top of each toast slice generously with cheese. Place soup servings under a broiler until cheese melts and browns. Makes 6 to 8 servings.

Mexican Albondigas Soup

Little meatballs and a touch of dry Sherry distinguish this consommé. Serve small portions as a first course, or as suggested below as a main dish.

- 1 pound ground beef
- ¾ teaspoon salt
- ¾ teaspoon chile powder
- 1 small onion, grated
- 1 cup fine dry bread crumbs
- ½ cup pine nuts
- 1 egg, slightly beaten
- 2 cans (10½ oz. *each*) condensed beef consommé
- 2 soup cans water
- 1 bay leaf
- ¼ cup **dry Sherry**

Mix together ground beef, salt, chile powder, onion, bread crumbs, pine nuts, and eggs in a mixing bowl. Shape into tiny meatballs each about 1-inch diameter. Pour consommé, water, and bay leaf into a saucepan; cover and bring to a boil. Add meatballs, a few at a time so that boiling is constant. Reduce heat, cover, and simmer for 30 minutes. Just before serving, remove bay leaf and stir in the Sherry. Serve in wide-rimmed soup bowls. Makes 6 servings.

Cream of Clam Broth

Use a crisp wine such as a Johannisberg Riesling.

- 3 dozen medium-sized clams
- 4 large shallots, or green onions including part of tops, chopped
- 1 large onion, chopped
- 1½ cups **dry white wine**
- 1 tablespoon chopped parsley
- Fresh ground pepper to taste
- Dash liquid hot pepper seasoning
- 3 cups whipping cream
- 2 egg yolks, beaten
- Dash paprika

Scrub the clams and put into a heavy pan with shallots, onion, wine, parsley, pepper, and dash liquid hot pepper seasoning. Cover and place over low heat. Let simmer 20 minutes. Remove clams and discard shells; set clams aside. Strain the liquid through several layers of cheesecloth. Reheat liquid, then add whipping cream and bring just to a boil; remove from heat and very gradually stir 1 cup of the hot broth with eggs then return all to pot. Correct seasoning to taste, adding necessary salt. Stir in reserved clams and serve hot or chilled. Garnish each serving with a dash of paprika. Makes 6 servings.

Salads

Pretty molded salads and colorful fruit bowls both benefit when wine is an ingredient. The fruit bowls, with simple wine-syrup, can often double as salads or desserts.

In vegetable salads, wine blends with the dressings. Noticeably absent is a green salad. Vinegar used in dressing has a discordant effect when served with wine. However, if you use lemon juice in its place with a favorite dressing, serve it confidently with any wine course.

Ruby Salad

This make-ahead molded salad combines elements of fresh fruit salad and cranberry relish. Serve it with the main course perhaps with turkey for Thanksgiving. Use Ruby Port or a wine such as Burgundy.

- 1 package (3 oz.) raspberry flavored gelatin
- 1 cup boiling water
- ½ cup **Ruby Port** or **dry red wine**
- 1 tablespoon lemon juice
- 1 can (1 lb.) whole cranberry sauce
- 1 teaspoon grated orange peel
- 1 cup halved, seeded red grapes
- Salad greens
- Mayonnaise or sour cream (optional)

Add gelatin to boiling water in a bowl and stir until dissolved. Add wine and lemon juice and stir until blended. Set in a pan of ice water and stir until slightly thick, about 20 minutes. Add cranberry sauce, orange peel, and halved grapes; mix until blended. Pour into a 1-quart mold or into 4 to 6 individual molds. Chill to firm.

Unmold to serve and garnish with salad greens. Pass mayonnaise or sour cream. Makes about 4 to 6 servings.

Spicy Green Bean Salad

The dressing for this zestful salad calls for both wine and wine vinegar. Use a wine such as a Burgundy or a Zinfandel.

- 2 cans (1 lb. *each*) cut green beans
- 1 medium-sized mild onion, thinly sliced
- ½ green pepper, thinly sliced
- ½ cup thinly sliced celery
- ⅛ teaspoon *each* oregano and dill weed or basil
- 1 clove garlic, mashed
- ½ teaspoon salt
- Dash pepper
- ¼ cup *each* wine vinegar and **dry red wine**
- ⅓ cup olive oil or salad oil
- Salad greens

Drain beans well and put into a bowl with the sweet onion, green pepper, and celery. Sprinkle in the oregano and dill or basil. In a small jar, combine the garlic, salt, pepper, vinegar, red wine, and olive oil; shake to combine, and pour over the beans. Mix lightly, cover bowl, and refrigerate about 2 hours, stirring gently several times. Serve on salad greens, if desired. Makes 4 to 6 servings.

Boysenberry Nut Salad

Frozen berries are the base of this molded salad.

- 1 package (10 oz.) frozen boysenberries
- Water
- 1 package (3 oz.) lemon flavored gelatin
- ¼ cup **medium Sherry**
- 1 small can (6 oz.) evaporated milk, chilled
- ½ cup chopped walnuts
- Salad greens
- Sour cream
- Sugar

Thaw boysenberries; drain and reserve the liquid. Measure boysenberry liquid and add enough water to make 1 cup. Heat the 1 cup liquid to boiling in a saucepan and add the lemon gelatin, stirring until dissolved. Add Sherry. Cool, then chill until thick and syrupy (about 30 minutes). Whip the chilled evaporated milk until stiff and fold into gelatin mixture. Fold in the boysenberries and nuts. Turn into a 1-quart salad mold or 8 individual molds (½-cup size). Chill until firm, at least 2 hours. Unmold onto serving plate, garnish with crisp greens, and serve with a dollop of plain sour cream or sour cream sweetened to taste. Makes 6 to 8 servings.

Fresh Strawberries and Wine

- 4 cups sliced fresh strawberries
- ½ cup **Ruby Port wine**

Put fresh sliced strawberries in a large bowl. Pour the wine over them and chill 2 to 3 hours to mingle flavors. Spoon into small bowls with juice and serve. Makes 4 to 6 servings.

Pineapple with Wine

Use a wine such as a sweet Sauterne or an apple wine.

- 1 large pineapple
- ½ cup **sweet white wine** or **fruit wine**
- ¼ cup shredded coconut

Cut pineapple in half lengthwise and hollow out all the fruit in chunks, preserving the shell. Sprinkle wine over pineapple chunks and chill about 1 hour, stirring occasionally. Spoon back into the shell and sprinkle shredded coconut over top. Makes 4 to 5 servings.

Summer Multifruit Bowl

Serve this fruit salad in a glass bowl for a most attractive presentation. Use a wine such as a Rhine or a Green Hungarian, or a less dry wine such as a sweet Sauterne.

- ½ cup sugar
- ¼ cup water
- 10 cups fresh fruit (cherries, grapes, strawberries, peaches, apricots, and plums)
- 1 cup **white wine**

Combine sugar and water in a saucepan and bring to a boil, stirring until sugar is dissolved; chill. Wash selected fruit and dry thoroughly. Stem and pit cherries, cut seedless grapes into small bunches, leave strawberries whole, peel peaches and cut in slices (dip in lemon juice if fruit must stand 30 minutes or longer before serving); halve and slice apricots and plums. Chill wine and fruit separately. Just before serving, arrange fruit in a bowl; pour chilled sugar syrup and wine over fruit and serve. Makes 10 to 12 servings.

Marinated Mushroom and Artichoke Salad

Prepare the salad early in the day and it will be ready to serve for dinner.

- 1 pound medium-sized mushrooms
- Boiling salted water
- 1 package (8 oz.) frozen artichoke hearts
- ⅓ cup chopped green onions, including part of the tops
- 1 small jar (2 oz.) pimiento-stuffed green olives, drained and sliced
- 1 tablespoon chopped pimiento
- ½ cup *each* olive oil and white wine vinegar
- 1 tablespoon **dry Sherry**
- ½ teaspoon salt
- ¼ teaspoon *each* garlic salt, oregano, and cracked pepper
- Salad greens

Wash, trim, and cut mushrooms into quarters. Drop into the boiling, salted water; boil 1 minute, drain and place into a bowl. Cook artichokes as directed on the package just until tender; drain and add to the mushrooms. Add the onions, olives, and pimientos.

For the dressing combine the oil, vinegar, Sherry, salt, garlic salt, oregano, and pepper; mix until blended, then pour over the vegetables. Cover and marinate at least 4 hours in the refrigerator, stirring several times. Arrange salad on crisp greens to serve. Makes about 6 servings.

Homemade Wine Vinegar

Homemade wine vinegar can add a special tang to salads and it is fun to make. Only three ingredients are required to prepare wine vinegar at home—dry wine, water, and wine vinegar culture*. The procedure is quite simple.

1.) Choose a small-mouthed glass, ceramic, or stainless steel container that will be no more than two-thirds filled by the vinegar mixture (contact with air is essential for culture action). Wash the container, rinse, fill with boiling water, then drain well.

2.) Combine in the container 1 part vinegar culture, 2 parts wine, and 1 part water. Close opening with a wad of sterile cotton.

3.) Set mixture in a warm place (ideally 80° to 90°) where temperature is fairly constant—near the hot water heater is a good spot. Let stand two to three months, or longer if the room is cooler.

When the wine vinegar is ready it tastes very acidic and has no alcohol flavor or aroma. (Commercial wine vinegar is about 5% acetic acid; homemade vinegar is about 8%.) There are three possible ways to deal with the finished wine vinegar:

1.) *Use it as is* or dilute for a more mellow taste with an equal amount of water, wine, or a combination of water and wine. Pour vinegar through muslin or nylon stocking to remove any sediment.

2.) *Preserve it* with a simple pasteurization. Heat vinegar 140° to 150° over direct heat or in a hot water bath. If you plan to dilute the wine vinegar with more wine, pasteurize the vinegar after you add the wine. Pour into sterilized bottles, close tightly, store at room temperature.

3.) *Make more vinegar* by using a portion of your first batch as starter and adding dry wine and water as indicated in the original recipe. Set aside for another two to three months. Use only unpasteurized wine vinegar for starter.

To make herb-flavored vinegars using tarragon, oregano, basil, dill, thyme, or other herb, immerse freshly cut sprigs (or dried herb) in the vinegar. Let stand until the vinegar takes on the desired flavor, then use. If you want to hold the flavor at a certain level, take out the herb, or pour the vinegar through a strainer.

To make garlic, onion, or shallot-flavored vinegars, add the chopped vegetable to the vinegar; let stand one to two weeks or until as strongly flavored as desired. Pour through a strainer and discard the vegetable.

**For information about obtaining wine vinegar culture write: Wine Products, Wine Vinegar Division, Box 732, Sausalito, California 94965.*

MEAT AND WINE COMBINATIONS

Ideas for Beef, Veal, Pork, Lamb

Meats can marinate, simmer, be basted with, or glazed by wine. In every step of preparation a use for wine can be found. Beef takes well to heartier full-bodied wine, while lamb and pork pair best with lighter reds to whites. But there is no hard and fast rule, and white wines have their role, too. Wine also flavors the sauce or gravy used with some of the meats.

Marinating with Wine

For centuries cooks have been aware of the tenderizing effects of wine on meat. The acid component of wine slowly breaks down meat tissues and fibers and adds a good, winey flavor in the process to meat. Marinating is especially popular for inexpensive cuts of meat, although the finer cuts benefit by contact with wine, too. Marinate small pieces of meat or poultry one or two hours (overnight for large pieces of meat) in a dry wine to cover in a glass or ceramic container. Turn several times. Seasonings such as garlic, onion, whole black pepper, herbs or spices may be added to the wine marinade. The meat can then be barbecued, broiled, braised, or roasted. Save some of the marinade for basting the meat as it cooks.

De-glazing with Wine

When you deglaze the pan in which you roast or sauté meat use a wine of your choice to make the sauce or gravy. To make a sauce after roasting or sautéing meat, remove accumulated fat and gradually add red or white wine or dry Sherry to the pan juices. Scrape all bits of meat into the sauce as it simmers. For gravies, make a smooth paste of 2 tablespoons each flour and water then blend well with pan juices before adding the wine.

Simmering with Wine

Simmering meat in wine works the same tenderizing magic as marinating. Long, slow simmering over low heat in wine for braised roasts or meat stews imparts flavor and softens the texture.

Basting with Wine

Spoon wine over meat as it roasts to give added flavor and to add to the meat's natural juices. This is an especially good idea for roasts such as beef, pork, and lamb.

Skirt Steaks Teriyaki

Marinate these skirt steak pinwheels overnight to absorb ample teriyaki flavor.

- 1 teaspoon unseasoned meat tenderizer
- 6 to 8 skirt steak pinwheels
- ¼ cup *each* **dry Sherry** and soy sauce
- ¼ teaspoon *each* ground ginger and garlic powder
- Dash pepper

Rub tenderizer into both sides of each steak; place in a shallow container. Combine Sherry, soy sauce, ginger, garlic powder, and pepper; pour over meat. Cover and chill for several hours or overnight, turning several times. Barbecue 6 to 8 inches over hot glowing coals 6 to 8 minutes on each side, or until steaks are of desired doneness. Makes 6 to 8 servings.

Parmesan-Crusted Swiss Steak

Long, slow cooking in a seasoned wine sauce tenderizes top round steak. Then you finish it off with golden, broiler-glazed topping of Parmesan cheese and mayonnaise dressing. Use a wine such as a Chablis or a dry Sauterne.

- 2½ pounds top round steak, cut 2 inches thick
- 2 tablespoons all-purpose flour
- 1 teaspoon seasoned salt
- ½ teaspoon *each* paprika and instant coffee powder
- ⅛ teaspoon garlic powder
- 2 tablespoons shortening
- ¼ cup finely chopped or thinly sliced onion
- ½ cup *each* canned condensed bouillon and **dry white wine**
- 1 teaspoon cornstarch blended with 1 teaspoon water
- ½ cup grated or shredded Parmesan cheese
- 2 tablespoons mayonnaise

Score steak on both sides, making diagonal cuts about ½ inch deep. Mix flour, seasoned salt, paprika, coffee powder, and garlic powder. Rub well into both sides of meat.

Heat shortening in a heavy frying pan with cover. Brown meat well on both sides in shortening over moderate heat. Drain off excess fat. Add onion, bouillon, and wine. Cover pan tightly, and simmer meat until tender, about 1½ hours. Remove meat to a metal tray and keep warm. Skim excess fat from juices remaining in the pan. Thicken with cornstarch and water to make gravy, if desired. Blend cheese and mayonnaise; spread over meat. Broil until glazed and brown. Serve steak with gravy in a side dish, if desired. Makes 6 servings.

Steak with Crab

Use a wine such as dry Semillon or dry Vermouth.

- 1½ pounds cross rib, sirloin tip, or boneless chuck steak, sliced ½ inch thick
- Unseasoned meat tenderizer
- 3 tablespoons butter or margarine
- ¼ teaspoon tarragon
- 6 ounces fresh, frozen, or canned crab
- ⅓ cup **dry white wine** or **dry Vermouth**
- 1 avocado
- ¼ cup sour cream
- 1 lemon, cut in wedges

Cut meat into 4 serving-sized pieces and rub meat tenderizer into both sides of meat. Heat 1 tablespoon of the butter in a large frying pan over medium-high heat and add steaks. Sprinkle steaks with tarragon. Sauté quickly until browned on one side, about 2 to 3 minutes, turn, and brown other side, cooking to desired doneness. Remove to hot platter and keep warm.

Add 1 more tablespoon butter to pan with crab meat and heat until hot through; spoon crab mixture over steaks. Add wine and remaining 1 tablespoon butter to pan drippings and heat, stirring until blended. Spoon over crab and steak. Peel and slice avocado and garnish each steak with 2 to 3 slices. Spoon a sour cream dollop on each steak and garnish with lemon wedges. Makes 4 servings.

Beef Rib Roast with Madeira Sauce

Serve a rich Madeira sauce with this well roasted piece of beef.

- 2 to 3-rib roast (6 to 8 lbs.)
- 1 teaspoon *each* salt and freshly ground pepper or to taste
- 1 can (10½ oz.) canned condensed beef consommé
- ¼ cup **Madeira**
- 1 tablespoon butter

Rub surface of the rib roast with salt and pepper. Insert a meat thermometer into thickest part of meat, being careful not to touch bone, and place on a rack in a roasting pan. Roast in a 325° oven, allowing about 20 minutes to the pound for rare meat (or until meat thermometer reaches 120° to 130°); or about 25 minutes per pound for medium-rare (140° to 150°).

To serve, place meat on a carving board. Pour off accumulated fat from roasting pan, reserving crusty drippings. Pour the consommé and Madeira into the pan and bring to a boil, scraping up drippings. Add butter and heat to melt. Pour into a sauce dish and pass to spoon over meat. Makes 6 to 8 servings.

Marinated London Broil

London broil originally indicated a way flank steak was cooked and served, and this recipe follows those guidelines. The thinly sliced rare meat is juicy and tender, well flavored by a wine marinade. (Nowadays, you also see various cuts of beef labeled London Broil.) Use a wine such as a Burgundy or a Zinfandel.

- ⅔ cup **dry red wine**
- ⅔ cup olive oil or salad oil
- 1 tablespoon soy sauce
- ⅛ teaspoon *each* oregano, marjoram, and pepper
- 1 large flank steak (1¼ to 1¾ lb.)
- Steamed wild rice and white rice

Mix together the wine, oil, soy sauce, and herbs. Place the flank steak in a deep bowl and pour marinade over the meat. Cover and chill at least 12 to 18 hours, turning meat once or twice.

Drain meat and broil 4 inches from heat about 5 minutes on each side. Cut meat in thin slices across the grain diagonally to top surface of steak; reserve juices. Spoon meat juices into cooked white rice and wild rice, mix lightly, and serve with meat. Makes about 4 servings.

Oven Rump Roast

Use a wine such as a Burgundy or a Gamay.

- 6-pound boneless rump roast
- 2 teaspoons salt
- 1 teaspoon dry mustard
- ¼ teaspoon *each* garlic salt and pepper
- Unseasoned meat tenderizer (optional)
- 1 tablespoon catsup
- 1 teaspoon Worcestershire
- ½ cup **dry red wine**

Rub the roast with salt, mustard, garlic salt, and pepper. (Use meat tenderizer as directed on package, if desired.) Insert meat thermometer into center of thickest part of roast, and place on a rack in a shallow baking pan.

Mix together catsup, Worcestershire, and wine; brush meat with this basting sauce. Roast in a 325° oven about 1 hour and 45 minutes or until meat thermometer registers 130° for rare (cook 18 minutes per pound). Baste with wine sauce several times during roasting; use all the sauce.

Let meat stand at room temperature 10 minutes to set juices, then slice and serve. Skim pan drippings of fat and serve with meat. Makes 10 servings.

Dutch Steak

Dutch chefs offer this variation of veal Cordon Bleu using beef steak, Canadian bacon, and Gouda cheese glazed with red wine. Use a wine such as a Claret or a Cabernet Sauvignon.

- 1½ pounds top sirloin steak, about ¾ inch thick, cut into 4 serving pieces
- ½ teaspoon *each* salt and garlic salt
- ¼ teaspoon *each* marjoram (crumbled) and freshly ground pepper
- 16 slices Canadian bacon (about ¼ lb.)
- 5 ounces Gouda cheese, thinly sliced
- 2 tablespoons butter or margarine
- 2 tablespoons chopped parsley
- ½ cup **dry red wine**
- 1 teaspoon beef stock base or 1 beef bouillon cube

Cut a slit-like pocket in one side of each steak serving, cutting to within ½ inch of the three other sides. Rub meat inside and out with a mixture of salt, garlic salt, marjoram, and pepper. Slip 2 slices each bacon and cheese inside meat pocket. Heat butter in a large frying pan and pan-fry meat over medium heat until nicely browned underneath. Turn and brown other side. Distribute remaining cheese slices on top of steak servings and cover each with 2 slices Canadian bacon.

Using a wide spatula and holding the top with a fork, quickly flip bacon-topped steaks over to heat and brown the bacon. Transfer to a hot platter, arranging servings bacon-side-up, sprinkle with parsley. Mix wine and beef stock base and pour into pan drippings; boil rapidly until reduced to a glaze. Spoon over meat. Makes 4 servings.

Steak Dijon on Toasted French Bread

Long a favorite businessman's lunch, the steak sandwich also makes a fine choice for a light supper. Wine sauce with Dijon-style mustard enhances the beef. Use a wine such as a Claret or a Cabernet Sauvignon.

1½ pounds top round steak (cut 1 inch thick)
2 tablespoons butter
¼ teaspoon *each* salt, garlic salt, and onion salt
1 teaspoon *each* beef broth and Dijon-style mustard
½ cup **dry red wine**
1 tablespoon *each* minced chives and parsley
Toasted French bread slices

Cut steak into 4 individual pieces. Pan fry each in butter over medium-high heat, turning to brown both sides, allowing about 3 minutes per side for rare. Season with salts.

Remove from pan and keep warm. Add beef broth, mustard, and wine to pan and cook on highest heat, stirring until reduced one-half. Spoon over steaks and sprinkle with chives and parsley. Serve on toasted French bread slices. Makes 4 servings.

Oven-Baked Stroganoff

Serve this simple stroganoff made with round steak over hot, cooked, buttered wide noodles. Use a wine such as a Burgundy or a Zinfandel.

2½ pounds top round steak, cut in thin strips
5 tablespoons salad oil or butter
1 large onion, thinly sliced
1 clove garlic, mashed
2 cups sliced fresh mushrooms
3 tablespoons all-purpose flour
1 teaspoon salt
¼ teaspoon pepper
¼ cup *each* **dry red wine** and tomato paste
1 bay leaf, crumbled
½ cup regular-strength beef broth or consommé
½ cup sour cream

In a frying pan brown strips of beef in 3 tablespoons of the oil; transfer meat to a 3-quart baking dish. Add remaining oil or butter to drippings in frying pan; sauté onion, garlic, and mushrooms until limp. Remove pan from heat and add flour, salt, pepper, wine, tomato paste, and bay leaf. Blend in beef broth. Stir until ingredients are blended. Pour over meat. Cover and bake in a 350° oven for 1 hour until meat is tender. Remove casserole from oven. Gently stir in sour cream and serve. Makes 6 servings.

Wine Beef and Onions

Strips of meat simmer until very tender in a tasty wine sauce with whole onions. Use a wine such as a Burgundy or a Zinfandel.

2 pounds boneless round steak (½ to ¾ inch thick), cut in strips 1 to 2 inches wide
2 cloves garlic, crushed
¼ teaspoon oregano
½ teaspoon basil
¼ teaspoon pepper
2 tablespoons salad oil
Juice of 1 lemon
1 tablespoon bacon drippings
1 bay leaf
8 small white onions, peeled
1½ tablespoons capers
½ teaspoon Worcestershire
1 cup **dry red wine**
¾ teaspoon salt
1 tablespoon minced fresh parsley

Spread garlic over strips of meat. Sprinkle with oregano, basil, and pepper. Place meat in a deep bowl and sprinkle with oil and lemon juice and marinate 1 hour. Brown beef in a large frying pan in the bacon drippings; then add bay leaf, whole onions, capers, Worcestershire, wine, and salt. Reduce heat, cover, and simmer 30 to 40 minutes, or until beef is tender. Transfer to serving dish, sprinkle with parsley. Makes 4 servings.

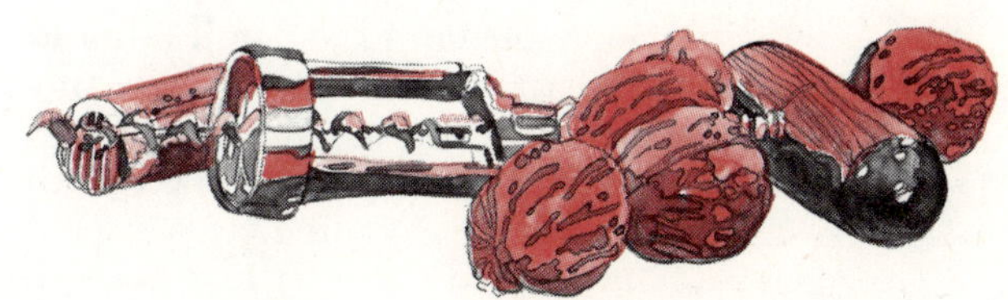

Beef à la Mode

This version of beef à la mode marinates up to 3 days, then cooks for 3 hours with several kinds of wine. Use a wine such as a Claret or a Cabernet Sauvignon along with the brandy and Madeira or Sherry.

- 6-pound beef rump roast
- 1 tablespoon salt
- Freshly ground pepper to taste
- 2 *each* medium-sized carrots, celery stalks, and onions, finely chopped
- ¼ cup chopped parsley
- 1 teaspoon thyme
- 2 cloves garlic, minced
- 3 cups **dry red wine**
- ¼ cup olive oil or salad oil
- ¼ cup **brandy** or **Cognac**
- 1 tablespoon butter or margarine
- 1 cracked veal knuckle or beef bone
- 3 tablespoons beef stock base
- About ½ cup water
- 1 tablespoon cornstarch
- 2 tablespoons **Madeira** or **Sherry**
- Watercress or parsley for garnish

Rub meat with salt and pepper and place in a deep, close fitting enamel, stainless steel, or earthenware bowl. Mix together carrots, celery, onions, parsley, thyme, garlic; sprinkle around and over meat. Pour in the red wine, 3 tablespoons of the olive oil, and brandy (the marinade should almost cover meat). Refrigerate for at least 24 hours, turning meat several times; you may refrigerate it up to 3 days.

Remove meat from marinade, drain, and pat dry with paper towels. Heat remaining 1 tablespoon of the oil and butter in a Dutch oven or deep casserole and brown meat well on all sides; pour off excess fat. Pour in wine marinade including chopped vegetables and let cook a few minutes to soften vegetables. Add knuckle, stock, and water. Bring to simmer, cover, and place in a 325° oven for 3 hours, or until meat is tender.

Transfer meat to a platter and keep warm. Remove and discard bones from broth and skim fat off. Strain broth through a wire strainer into a saucepan, pressing liquid out of vegetables. Discard vegetables. Bring wine liquid to a boil (should be about 3 cups; add water, if needed, to make this amount) and blend in a paste of cornstarch and Madeira or Sherry; stirring constantly, cook until thickened. Taste to correct seasoning.

Slice meat and arrange on a platter and garnish with watercress or parsley. Spoon part of the sauce over the meat and pass a bowl with remaining sauce. Makes 10 to 12 servings.

Pot Roast with Pasta

While this pot roast cooks slowly, rich flavored juices develop and make the sauce for the accompanying pasta. Use a wine such as a Chianti or a Barbera.

- 4 to 5-pound pot roast
- 1 teaspoon salt
- 1 tablespoon salad oil or shortening
- ½ cup *each* chopped carrots, celery, and onion
- 1 cup **dry red wine**
- 1 can (10½ oz.) condensed beef consommé
- 1 can (6 oz.) tomato paste
- 6 canned anchovy fillets, minced
- 1 bay leaf
- 2 cloves garlic, minced or mashed
- ½ pound mushrooms, sliced
- 2 tablespoons butter or margarine
- 1 package (8 to 12 oz.) spaghetti, cooked according to package directions, drained and hot

Sprinkle entire roast with salt and brown well on all sides in the heated salad oil in a Dutch oven. Add carrots, celery, and onion and continue cooking until slightly browned. Add wine, consommé, tomato paste, anchovies, bay and garlic. Cover; simmer slowly over low heat until meat is tender, about 3 hours.

Meanwhile, sauté mushrooms in butter until lightly browned; stir into sauce about ½ hour before meat is done. Remove meat to serving platter and simmer sauce, uncovered, until reduced to thickness you desire. Serve sauce over hot spaghetti with the sliced meat. Makes 10 to 12 servings.

Ground Beef in Mushroom Sauce

Sour cream or yogurt are alternate choices to finish this quick ground beef-style stroganoff.

- 1 small onion, chopped
- ¼ cup (⅛ lb.) butter or margarine
- 1½ pounds lean ground beef
- 1 small clove garlic, minced or mashed
- 1 teaspoon salt
- ⅛ teaspoon pepper
- 1 can (10½ oz.) condensed cream of chicken soup, undiluted
- ½ can (6 oz. size) tomato paste
- 1 can (6 or 8 oz.) sliced mushrooms, drained
- ¼ cup **dry Sherry**
- 1 cup (½ pt.) sour cream or yogurt
- Hot cooked noodles
- Chopped dill pickles

In a large frying pan, sauté onion in butter until golden. Add beef, break apart and cook, stirring, until it loses its pinkness. Stir in garlic, salt, pepper, chicken soup, and tomato paste. Add mushrooms and Sherry; mix until blended. Cover and simmer gently 15 minutes. Stir in sour cream or yogurt. Heat, but do not boil. Serve sauce over the noodles. Top with dill pickles. Makes about 6 servings.

Barbecued Cross-Rib Roast

You have the option of barbecuing this roast by several techniques or oven roasting it. Use a wine such as a Burgundy or a Pinot Noir.

- 4 to 5-pound boneless, tied, beef cross-rib roast
- ⅓ cup catsup
- ¾ cup **dry red wine**
- ½ cup salad oil
- 1 tablespoon instant minced onion
- 1 tablespoon Worcestershire
- 1 teaspoon crumbled rosemary
- 1½ teaspoons salt
- ¼ teaspoon pepper
- 5 drops liquid smoke seasoning (optional)

Set the beef in a deep, close fitting bowl. Blend together the catsup, wine, salad oil, onion, Worcestershire, rosemary, salt, pepper, and liquid smoke seasoning, if desired. Pour over the roast; if it does not cover meat, turn roast several times while marinating. Cover and refrigerate 12 to 24 hours. Lift meat from marinade and insert a meat thermometer into the center.

Cook roast on a rotisserie, in a covered barbecue, or in the oven, basting frequently with marinade. On a rotisserie, place meat 6 inches above medium-hot coals; medium coals in a covered barbecue; or set oven at 325°. All methods require about 1½ hours for rare meat. The thermometer should register 130° for rare; 140° for medium-rare to medium. Let roast stand about 20 minutes, then slice thinly and serve with meat juices. Makes 8 to 10 servings.

Sauerbraten

The spicy wine and vegetable marinade of this German entrée tenderizes and penetrates the meat over a period of two days, adding a lusty sweet-sour flavor. Potato pancakes are the traditional accompaniment. Use a wine such as Mountain Red or Zinfandel.

- 2 *each* medium-sized onions and carrots, minced
- 1 clove garlic, minced or mashed
- ½ cup chopped celery
- 6 whole black peppers
- 4 tablespoons olive oil or salad oil
- 1 cup red wine vinegar
- 2 cups **dry red wine**
- ¼ cup firmly packed brown sugar
- 1 tablespoon salt
- 1 bay leaf
- 1 tablespoon pickling spice (remove red pepper)
- 3 to 4-pound top round roast, beef rump, or sirloin tip roast
- 1 can (6 oz.) tomato paste
- 1 cup canned regular-strength beef broth
- 15 gingersnaps, crushed

In a frying pan sauté onions, carrots, garlic, celery, and pepper in 2 tablespoons of the oil until soft. Add wine vinegar, wine, brown sugar, salt, bay leaf, and pickling spice; allow to cool in a glass or ceramic bowl. When mixture is cool, submerge roast and marinate for two days, covered, in the refrigerator; turn frequently.

Remove meat from marinade, pat dry, and brown slowly in remaining 2 tablespoons oil in a Dutch oven. Pour off any excess fat and add marinade. Cover and simmer about 1 hour over low heat. Add tomato paste and beef broth; continue to cook until tender, about 2 hours.

Remove roast and keep warm; strain remaining sauce and vegetables through a wire strainer. Then boil until liquid is reduced by about a third. Add crushed gingersnaps, stir in well, reheat. Spoon gingersnap sauce over meat slices to serve. Makes 8 servings.

Oven-Simmered Beef Stew

A hearty wine helps develop a robust flavor in beef stew. Use a wine such as a Burgundy or a Zinfandel.

1½ pounds boneless beef chuck, cut into 1-inch cubes
1 package (4 to 6 serving size) dry onion soup mix
1 package (about ¾ oz.) mushroom gravy mix
⅛ teaspoon pepper
1 cup **dry red wine**
½ cup water
6 carrots, peeled and cut into ¾-inch pieces
3 medium-sized potatoes, peeled and cut in 1-inch cubes
½ pound mushrooms, sliced
Chopped fresh parsley (optional)

Place beef cubes in a 3-quart casserole with a tight-fitting lid. In a small bowl, combine onion soup mix, mushroom gravy mix, pepper, wine, and water. Pour over the meat. Cover casserole and bake in a 350° oven for about 1 hour.

Remove casserole from oven and stir in carrots, potatoes, and mushrooms. Cover and return to oven for about 1½ hours more, or until meat and vegetables are tender when pierced with a fork.

Remove from oven and sprinkle chopped parsley over the top before serving. Makes about 4 servings.

Oxtail Soup

Serve mashed potatoes or hot rice with each portion of this meaty soup. Use a white or red wine, either a Chablis or dry Sauterne, or a Burgundy or Zinfandel.

2 large onions, chopped
3 tablespoons salad oil
3 pounds oxtails, cut in 1-inch lengths
1 small bottle (⅘ qt.) or 1¾ cups **dry white** or **dry red wine**
1 can (14 oz.) regular-strength beef broth
1 can (6 oz.) tomato paste
2 medium-sized carrots, finely chopped
2 stalks celery, finely chopped
1 small turnip, finely chopped
1 teaspoon sugar
Salt to taste

In a large frying pan, sauté onions in 2 tablespoons of the oil until onions are limp. Place in a large pan (at least 4-qt. size). Add remaining 1 tablespoon oil to frying pan and brown oxtail pieces, a few at a time, adding meat to the pan as it is browned. Pour wine into frying pan and bring to boiling, scraping free all browned particles. Add wine to the soup pan along with the beef broth, tomato paste, vegetables, and sugar.

Cover and simmer over low heat for 2½ to 3 hours or until meat falls from bones and broth is very thick. Add salt to taste. (If made ahead and refrigerated, add ¼ cup beef broth or dry wine and reheat.) Makes 4 servings.

Boeuf Bourguignonne

This Sunset favorite combines Sherry and red wine with beef. Crusty French bread goes well here. Use a wine such as a Burgundy or a Mountain Red.

2 tablespoons butter or margarine
2 pounds boneless beef chuck, cut into 1-inch cubes
¼ cup **dry** or **medium Sherry**
½ pound medium-sized mushrooms, quartered
6 tablespoons all-purpose flour
2 teaspoons *each* catsup and bottled brown gravy sauce
2 cups water or regular-strength beef broth
2 cups **dry red wine**
1 bay leaf
1 teaspoon *fines herbes*
Salt and pepper to taste
1 can (1 lb.) small whole onions, drained

In a Dutch oven, melt butter over medium-high heat; add beef and brown. Pour Sherry over the beef, then remove meat from pan with slotted spoon. Add mushrooms to pan; cook, stirring, for 1 minute. Blend in flour, catsup, gravy sauce, and

water. Cook, stirring, until mixture begins to boil. Return meat to pan and add 1 cup of the wine, bay leaf, fine herbs, salt and pepper to taste. Cover pan and simmer 2 to 2½ hours, until meat is tender, adding remaining cup of wine, if needed. Stir occasionally. About 30 minutes before meat is done, add onions to heat and absorb flavors of the stew. Makes 4 to 6 servings.

Carne Con Garbanzos

This is a Mexican-style rendition of beef stew. Use a wine such as a Burgundy or a Gamay.

- 1 pound boneless beef stew, cut in 1-inch chunks
- About ⅓ cup all-purpose flour
- ¼ teaspoon celery salt
- 2 tablespoons salad oil
- 1 medium-sized onion, chopped
- 1 cup chopped celery
- 1 beef bouillon cube
- ½ cup hot water
- 1 can (about 1 lb.) garbanzos, drained
- ½ cup pitted ripe olives, drained
- ¾ cup canned whole tomatoes with juice
- ⅛ teaspoon whole oregano
- ½ teaspoon salt
- 2 whole cloves
- ⅔ cup **dry red wine**

Dust beef with flour and sprinkle with celery salt. Heat oil in heavy frying pan, and brown beef and onion. Add celery, bouillon cube, water, garbanzos, olives, tomatoes, oregano, salt, cloves, and ⅓ cup of the wine. Cover and simmer 1 hour; then add remaining wine and let simmer 1 more hour or until beef is tender. Makes 3 to 4 servings.

Swiss Julienne of Veal

The make-ahead character of this popular Swiss dish suits it to entertaining. Tenderized veal strips are sautéed then blended into a smooth wine cream sauce. The last minute dramatic addition is flaming brandy. Use a wine such as a Chablis or a Chardonnay.

- 2 pounds boneless veal cutlets cut ⅓ inch thick
- Salt, pepper, and paprika
- 3 tablespoons butter or margarine
- 2 tablespoons chopped shallots or green onions
- 3 tablespoons all-purpose flour
- 1 cup whipping cream
- ½ cup **dry white wine**
- ¼ cup **brandy**

Carefully trim away skin or fat from each cutlet then place one piece of veal at a time between two pieces of waxed paper and pound with a smooth-surfaced mallet to flatten evenly about ¼-inch thick. Sprinkle meat lightly on each side with salt, pepper, and paprika. Cut into strips ¼ inch wide and 1½ inches long.

In a wide frying pan heat butter until bubbly. Add shallots and sauté until just softened. Add veal strips and cook over medium-high heat, stirring frequently, until no longer pink, about 4 minutes. Remove meat and shallots to a 1-quart bowl. Stir the flour into drippings in pan; cook, stirring, until bubbly. Gradually blend in cream and white wine. Cook, stirring until thickened and smooth. (If you plan to serve later, cover and refrigerate the meat and sauce separately in covered containers.)

Shortly before serving, add cooked meats to hot sauce in a chafing dish. Cook, stirring frequently, about 5 minutes, or until heated through. Heat ¼ cup brandy just until warm to touch; ignite and pour over veal in sauce. Stir until flames die down, then serve. Makes about 6 servings.

Baekeoffe

This provincial Alsatian stew, rich in meaty juices, should be served in rimmed plates or wide soup bowls. Use a wine such as a Rhine, a Traminer, or a Gewürztraminer.

- 4 medium-sized boiling potatoes (about 1½ lbs.), peeled and cut in ¼-inch slices
- 1 pound *each* pork shoulder and veal shoulder, cut in 1-inch cubes
- 2 medium-sized onions, thinly sliced
- ⅓ cup finely chopped fresh parsley
- 2 cloves garlic, minced or mashed
- 2 bay leaves
- 1½ teaspoons salt
- ¼ teaspoon pepper
- 1 small bottle (⅘ qt.) or 1¾ cups **dry white wine**
- ¼ cup (⅛ lb.) butter or margarine

Lightly grease a 3 or 4-quart casserole; layer in half the potatoes; top with half the pork and half the veal; then add half the onions and half the parsley, 1 clove garlic and 1 bay leaf. Repeat with remaining potatoes, pork, veal, onions, parsley, and garlic, finishing with a bay leaf. Sprinkle salt and pepper over all; slowly pour in wine and lay butter pieces on top.

Cover and bake in a 375° oven for about 1½ hours until meat is tender. Makes 6 servings.

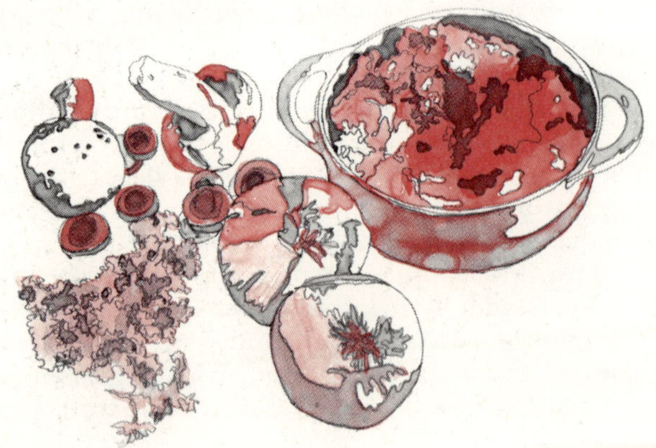

Veal Rolls with Sweet Wine Sauce

Delicate veal birds blend French and Italian cuisine. They are filled with a chicken, mushroom, and parsley filling and glazed with a sweet wine such as a sweet Sauterne or White Port.

- 1 whole chicken breast, split (about 1 lb.)
- ¼ cup water
- 1 teaspoon chicken stock base
- ¼ pound mushrooms
- 3 tablespoons butter
- 2 tablespoons *each* finely chopped onion and fresh parsley
- 2 tablespoons fine dry bread crumbs
- 2 egg yolks
- 8 boneless veal cutlets, cut ⅛ inch thick in 4 by 6-inch pieces (about 1⅓ lbs.)
- 2 tablespoons all-purpose flour
- 1 teaspoon salt
- ¼ teaspoon pepper
- 1 whole egg, slightly beaten
- 1 cup **sweet white wine**
- 2 teaspoons cornstarch
- 1 lemon, thinly sliced

Put chicken breasts, water, and chicken stock base in a small pan, cover and simmer gently for 20 minutes. Cool; discard skin and bones and dice meat, reserving broth. Slice 2 or 3 mushrooms thinly for garnish; finely chop remaining mushrooms. Melt 1 tablespoon of the butter and sauté the sliced mushrooms slightly and remove from pan. Add the chopped mushrooms and chopped onion and sauté for a few minutes, just until tender. Remove from heat. Add 1 tablespoon parsley, the diced chicken, bread crumbs, egg yolks, and reserved broth; mix well.

Spread some filling evenly over each cutlet and roll up; skewer with a toothpick. Mix together the flour, salt, and pepper and dust veal rolls lightly in it. Dip in the slightly beaten egg, then brown in the remaining melted butter, turning until golden brown. Pour in the wine, cover, and simmer 15 minutes, or until veal is tender to pierce.

Remove veal rolls to a serving platter. Blend cornstarch with 1 tablespoon water to make a paste and stir into the wine drippings; cook until thickened. Add the sautéed sliced mushrooms and reheat. Spoon mushroom wine sauce over veal rolls and sprinkle with remaining chopped parsley. Garnish with lemon. Makes 4 to 6 servings.

Veal Scallopini with Marsala

The conventional scallopini calls for Marsala or dry Sherry.

- ½ pound fresh medium-sized mushrooms
- 4 tablespoons (⅛ lb.) butter
- Juice of ½ lemon (1½ tablespoons lemon juice)
- 1½ pounds boneless veal round, cut ⅛ inch thick
- ¼ cup all-purpose flour
- 1 teaspoon salt
- ¼ teaspoon pepper
- ¾ cup **Marsala** or **dry Sherry**
- 1 teaspoon beef stock base or 1 bouillon cube
- 1 tablespoon minced parsley

Slice mushrooms thinly. Melt 2 tablespoons of the butter in a large frying pan, add mushrooms, sprinkle with lemon juice, and sauté for a few minutes, just until limp. Spoon out of pan and set aside.

Cut veal into strips about 1 inch wide and dust in flour seasoned with salt and pepper. Melt remaining butter in the frying pan and brown meat quickly, turning to brown both sides. Pour in wine, add beef stock and cook rapidly for a few minutes, stirring constantly. Return mushrooms to the pan and heat until hot through.

Garnish with minced parsley and serve at once. Makes 4 to 6 servings.

Baked Veal Chops

Each sautéed veal chop is covered with onion, Swiss cheese, and cracker crumbs before baking.

- 4 tablespoons butter
- 6 veal chops, with all skin and fat removed
- Salt and pepper
- ¼ teaspoon tarragon
- 1 large onion, thinly sliced
- 1 cup shredded domestic Swiss cheese
- ½ cup cracker crumbs
- ½ cup **White Port**
- ½ cup canned condensed beef consommé

In a frying pan that can go into the oven, melt 2 tablespoons of the butter and lightly brown veal chops on both sides. Remove from heat, salt and pepper lightly, and sprinkle with tarragon. Cover each chop with slices of onion, cover the onions with Swiss cheese, and top cheese evenly with cracker crumbs. Put a small piece of the remaining butter on top of each chop. Pour the White Port and consommé into the pan. Cover, place in a 350° oven, and bake 45 minutes until meat is very tender when pierced. Spoon extra liquid over chops when served. Makes 6 servings.

Veal Stew with Potato Soufflé

Use a wine such as a dry Sauterne or a dry Semillon.

- ½ pound chicken livers
- 2 tablespoons butter or margarine
- 2 pounds boneless veal stew meat, cut in 1-inch cubes
- ¾ cup *each* **dry white wine** and regular-strength chicken broth
- 1 teaspoon *each* salt and tarragon
- 8 carrots
- Instant mashed potatoes (amount for 4 servings)
- ¼ cup grated Parmesan cheese
- 3 eggs, separated
- 1 tablespoon cornstarch mixed with 1 tablespoon cold water
- 1 can (16 oz.) small whole onions, drained

Using a large pan, quickly brown chicken livers in butter, then remove from pan and reserve. Brown veal in remaining drippings, turning to brown all sides. Pour in wine and broth. Season with salt and tarragon. Peel carrots, trim ends, and halve if large. Add to the meat. Cover and simmer about 40 minutes, or until tender.

About 5 to 10 minutes before the cooking time is up, prepare instant mashed potatoes as directed on the package for 4 servings. Mix in cheese and with a spoon beat in egg yolks, one at a time. Beat egg whites until soft peaks form and fold into potatoes.

Blend cornstarch with cold water until smooth then blend into the stew meat juices; simmer 2 or 3 minutes, stirring. Add sautéed chicken livers and onions and transfer stew to a 2-quart soufflé dish or other round baking dish. Spoon soufflé mixture over the hot stew. Place in a 375° oven and bake 30 minutes, or until potatoes are puffed and set. Makes 6 to 8 servings.

Veal Zucchini

A colorful selection of red and green vegetables blend refreshingly with the veal. Use a dry white wine such as Mountain White or Chablis.

- About 2 tablespoons butter
- 2 pounds veal chops or cutlets
- 2 medium-sized onions, chopped
- 1 clove garlic
- 1 can (1 lb.) whole tomatoes
- ½ cup **dry white wine**
- ½ teaspoon chopped fresh oregano (or ¼ teaspoon dried)
- ½ teaspoon *each* Italian seasoning mix and savory
- Salt and pepper to taste
- 2 beef bouillon cubes
- 4 medium-sized zucchini, thinly sliced
- 1 bunch fresh spinach, rinsed, drained, and coarsely chopped
- Hot cooked rice or noodles

Heat butter in a large frying pan over medium-high heat. Quickly brown veal and remove from pan; set aside. In the same pan, sauté the onions and garlic until soft, adding more butter if needed. Add tomatoes (slightly crushed), wine, oregano, Italian seasoning, savory, salt, pepper, and bouillon cubes. Cover and simmer 30 minutes; remove lid, turn heat to high, and reduce the liquid to half.

Reduce heat to simmer, add zucchini and veal, including any meat juices, cover and simmer 7 minutes, or until zucchini is tender. Add spinach, cover, and cook 3 more minutes. Turn into a heated serving dish. Serve with rice or noodles. Makes 4 to 6 servings.

Veal Chalet

Asparagus, avocado, and tomatoes are part of this hot tiered sandwich. Veal, simmered tender with wine and lemon, is the base. Use a wine such as a Chablis or a Green Hungarian.

- 2 boneless veal round steaks (about 1 lb.)
- Salt
- All-purpose flour
- 1 egg, well-beaten
- About ¼ cup fine dry bread crumbs
- ¼ cup butter or margarine
- ⅓ cup **dry white wine**
- ½ lemon, thinly sliced
- 4 slices firm-textured white bread, toasted
- 4 slices tomato
- 8 slices avocado
- 8 cooked asparagus spears (hot or cold)
- About 1 cup shredded soft jack cheese
- Paprika

Trim membrane from veal, cut each steak in half and sprinkle with salt. Turn meat in flour, shaking off excess. Dip each piece in egg then coat evenly with bread crumbs. Melt butter in a wide frying pan over medium-high heat. Add veal pieces and brown on all sides. Add to the pan the wine and lemon; cover and simmer gently for about 20 minutes or until the meat is quite tender to pierce.

Place each piece of meat on a slice of toast. Top each with 1 slice tomato, 2 slices avocado, 2 asparagus spears (add salt if needed), and about ¼ cup of the cheese. Broil until top is bubbling. Sprinkle each sandwich with paprika and serve. Makes 4 servings.

Pork

Ham Steaks

These ham steaks develop a smoky-sweet flavor blending the barbecue effects and the wine-jelly-mustard sauce. Use a wine such as Vin Rosé or Gamay Rosé.

- 2 center-cut ham steaks, ¾ to 1 inch thick
- ½ cup currant jelly
- ½ cup **Rosé**
- 1 tablespoon prepared mustard

Grill the ham over a rather hot fire, high enough above the coals so steaks don't burn. Cook about 30 to 45 minutes turning frequently until nicely browned on all sides.

While steaks cook, heat the jelly, wine, and mustard in a small pan until the jelly is thoroughly melted. When steaks are browned well, put side by side in a shallow pan and pour the jelly mixture over them. Cover and allow to simmer gently about 30 minutes on a cool part of the grill. Cut each steak into two or three pieces and serve with some sauce over each. Makes 4 to 6 servings.

Ham in Pastry

This canned ham is *en croute* or baked in pastry, but is first surrounded by a mushroom stuffing, and resembles the French *jambon en croute*. It can be completely assembled a day in advance.

- 4 cups water
- 4 tablespoons beef stock base
- 1 cup **Madeira** or **Ruby Port**
- 1 carrot, peeled and chopped
- 1 medium-sized onion, chopped
- 5- to 6-pound canned ham
- 3 tablespoons butter or margarine
- 1 pound mushrooms, chopped
- Juice of ½ lemon, about 1½ tablespoons
- 3 tablespoons instant minced onions
- 2 green onions, including part of tops, chopped
- ¼ teaspoon *each* salt, thyme, and allspice
- Freshly ground pepper
- 1 can (2 or 3 oz.) liver pâté
- ½ cup fine dry bread crumbs
- Pastry (recipe follows)
- 1 egg yolk
- 1 tablespoon water

Using a large pan or Dutch oven, bring to a boil the 4 cups water with the stock base, wine, chopped carrot, and onion. Add the ham, cover, and simmer gently for 1 hour; remove from broth and let drain; cool. Reserve broth.

Meanwhile, melt butter in a large frying pan, add mushrooms, sprinkle with lemon juice and cook until limp and juices evaporate. Add all onions, salt, thyme, allspice, and pepper. Remove from heat and stir in pâté and bread crumbs. Cool.

Roll out pastry about ⅜ inch thick to a rectangle large enough to enclose the meat (about 14 by 18 inches).

Spread the mushroom filling over the pastry, pressing in firmly, leaving a 1½-inch margin on all sides. Place meat, top side down, with the long side of ham across the short side of pastry center. Wrap pastry around meat and seal securely down middle and at ends, moistening pastry edges with water. Place seam side down, on a greased baking sheet and garnish with designs cut from pastry scraps.

Brush pastry with a mixture of 1 egg yolk beaten with 1 tablespoon water. Bake in a 400° oven 30 minutes until browned. Cut into ½-inch-thick slices, and serve hot with the strained, unthickened reserved stock.

Pastry:

Stir together 2½ cups sifted regular all-purpose flour and 1 teaspoon salt. Cut in ¾ cup (⅜ lb.) butter until all particles are of uniform texture. Beat 3 egg yolks with 3 tablespoons water and mix into flour with a fork, then stir to blend dough until it sticks together; add 1 more tablespoon water if needed. Press dough into a compact ball, cover, and chill.

Flemish-Style Ham

First, the ham absorbs flavor in a marinade, then to further emphasize the seasonings it simmers in the same liquid. Use a wine such as Chablis or a Sauvignon Blanc.

- 4 to 6-pound boneless, cooked ham
- 1¾ cups (⅖ qt.) **dry white wine**
- 2 cloves garlic, minced or mashed
- 2 bay leaves
- 6 whole cloves
- 6 sprigs parsley
- 1 teaspoon thyme
- 2 tablespoons butter or margarine
- 1 medium-sized onion, sliced
- 2 large carrots, sliced
- 2 tablespoons sugar
- 3 tablespoons *each* all-purpose flour and water

Place ham in a deep bowl. Combine wine with garlic, bay, cloves, parsley, and thyme; pour over ham. Marinate for 3 to 6 hours, turning several times. Remove ham from marinade, pat dry; save marinade. Using a Dutch oven over medium heat, brown ham well on all sides. About halfway through browning, add butter, onion, and carrots to pan and sprinkle with sugar. Cook, stirring vegetables and turning meat, until both are richly browned, about 20 minutes. Add marinade to pan; cover, and simmer for 1 hour.

Lift ham from pan to a serving platter; pour cooking liquid through a wire strainer, discarding vegetables. Blend flour and water smoothly and stir into cooking liquid; boil, stirring, until thickened; serve in a bowl to spoon over ham. Makes 8 to 12 servings.

Barbecued Country-Style Spareribs

Thick, meaty country-style spareribs should be cooked slowly over low heat. A barbecue with a lid or hood fashioned of foil captures the smoke flavor. Use a wine such as a Chablis or a dry Sauterne.

1 cup *each* catsup, water, and **dry white wine**
¼ cup Worcestershire
1 medium-sized onion, sliced
1 whole lemon, thinly sliced
1 clove garlic, sliced
2 tablespoons butter or margarine
4 pounds country-style spareribs
Salt and pepper

Combine catsup, water, wine, Worcestershire, onion, lemon, garlic, and butter in a large frying pan or other pan large enough to hold the 4 pounds spareribs. Bring to boiling, reduce heat, cover, and simmer slowly for 30 minutes. Add spareribs. This much can be done ahead.

Lift meat from sauce and sprinkle all sides with salt and pepper. Place fat side up on the grill about 4 to 6 inches over the slowly burning barbecue coals. Put lid on barbecue and adjust drafts to keep coals burning slowly.

Cook 1 hour to 1 hour 20 minutes, turning several times. Use 1 cup of the barbecue sauce for basting and baste often. Reheat the remaining sauce in pan.

Remove ribs from the grill when they have lost all pink color in thickest portion close to bone (cut a gash to test). Cut into individual servings, and put them into the heated sauce. Cover pan of sauce and meat and simmer 20 to 30 minutes. When you serve the spareribs, spoon some of the sauce over each piece. Makes about 6 servings.

Pork with Red Cabbage

Pork and cabbage, as prepared in this dish, hails from the Lorraine region of France. It makes a complete meal in itself, braised with apples and red wine. Use a wine such as a Burgundy or a Zinfandel.

3½ teaspoons salt
¾ teaspoon thyme
¼ teaspoon *each* pepper and allspice
½ teaspoon crushed bay leaf
3 cloves garlic
3-pound boneless, rolled pork loin roast
¼ cup butter or margarine
1 onion, thinly sliced
½ cup chopped carrots
1 medium-sized head (about 2 lbs.) red cabbage, shredded
2 unpeeled tart apples, diced
2 tablespoons vinegar
⅛ teaspoon nutmeg
1 tablespoon *each* butter or margarine and salad oil
1 cup **dry red wine**

Mix together 3 teaspoons of the salt, the thyme, pepper, allspice, ¼ teaspoon of the crushed bay leaf, and 1 clove of the garlic, finely crushed. Rub into meat, distributing evenly. Cover meat, refrigerate, and let stand for 2 hours or overnight. Scrape off seasonings, and pat meat dry with paper towels. Melt the ¼ cup butter in a very large frying pan; add onion, carrots, and remaining 2 cloves garlic, crushed, and cook slowly until vegetables are soft but not browned. Add cabbage, stirring until slightly limp. Mix in apples, vinegar, remaining ¼ teaspoon bay leaf, nutmeg, and remaining ½ teaspoon salt. Spoon mixture around the inside edge of a large oval baking dish (4 to 6 qts.) that can be tightly covered.

Brown pork well on all sides in the 1 tablespoon butter and oil. Place roast in center of cabbage in baking dish. Insert meat thermometer in center of roast. Heat wine until simmering; pour over meat and cabbage. Cover baking dish and bake in a 325° oven for about 1½ hours, or until meat thermometer reaches 170°.

Remove string around meat and cut in ½-inch slices. Arrange drained cabbage around meat on serving plate. Skim fat from cooking juices; boil juices down quickly to a sauce consistency. Serve separately to spoon over meat and cabbage. Makes 6 to 8 servings.

Sherried Pork Chops and Pears

Winter pears and pork chops, baked together, make an attractive casserole.

6 to 8 center-cut pork chops (*each* about ¾ inch thick)
Salt
3 or 4 firm, ripe Anjou pears
2 tablespoons lemon juice
¼ cup firmly packed brown sugar
½ teaspoon cinnamon
¼ cup **dry Sherry**
1 tablespoon butter
½ teaspoon *each* cornstarch and water

Trim most of the fat from the chops and heat a little of the pork fat in a wide frying pan, stirring, until pan is lightly greased. Add pork chops, without crowding, and brown well on all sides over moderate heat. Sprinkle meat lightly with salt and arrange chops on one side of a shallow casserole.

Cut pears in halves lengthwise, core, and remove stem and blossom end. Set pears, cut side up, beside pork; sprinkle meat and fruit with lemon juice. Mix brown sugar and cinnamon, distribute over meat and fruit, then pour Sherry over all. Put a dot of butter in each pear hollow. Cover casserole and bake in a 350° oven for 40 minutes; after the first 20 minutes remove cover.

When casserole has baked, spoon or siphon out pan juices and transfer to a small pan. Blend cornstarch and water, then add to pan juices; bring to a boil, stirring. Pour sauce over pork and pears and serve. Makes 6 to 8 servings.

Lamb

Butterflied Barbecued Leg of Lamb

A whole bottle of wine is the base of the marinade for this leg of lamb. Use a wine such as a Mountain White or Chablis.

1 large leg of lamb, about 6½ to 7 pounds with bone in
2 teaspoons salt
½ teaspoon pepper
1½ tablespoons *each* curry powder and whole oregano
1 tablespoon minced garlic
1 bottle (⅘ qt.) **dry white wine**

Bone and butterfly the lamb, or have your meatman do it. (To butterfly, you cut partially through thickest portion of boned leg, spreading out to make a fairly even layer.) Combine salt, pepper, curry, oregano, and garlic, and rub all over the meat. Put the meat in a close fitting bowl, and pour in wine. Marinate 5 to 6 hours or overnight; turn occasionally.

Lift meat from marinade and place on the barbecue grill about 4 inches over hot fire and brown quickly on both sides. Then move farther away from fire (or spread out coals to reduce heat) and slowly cook for 45 minutes to 1 hour or until meat thermometer inserted in thickest portion registers 140° for medium-rare. Turn occasionally to cook evenly, basting as needed with remaining marinade. Slice to serve. Makes 8 to 10 servings.

Sirloin Lamb Chops with Mandarin Sauce

Broiled sirloin lamb chops are crowned with mandarin orange slices in a Cumberland-style sauce.

3 tablespoons currant jelly
⅓ cup orange juice
½ cup **Ruby Port**
2 tablespoons lemon juice
1 teaspoon dry mustard
½ teaspoon ground ginger
½ teaspoon cornstarch blended with 1 tablespoon cold water
4 sirloin lamb chops (about 2 lbs.)
Salt and pepper
1 can (11 oz.) mandarin oranges, drained

In a small pan, heat together the jelly, orange juice, wine, lemon juice, mustard, and ginger, stirring until flavors are blended and sauce is hot through. Blend cornstarch with water to make a paste and stir into hot wine mixture; stirring, cook until thickened and translucent.

Season lamb chops with salt and pepper and broil 3 to 4 inches from heat for about 4 minutes on a side for rare, or to desired doneness. Transfer meat to a serving platter. Add oranges to wine sauce, heat until hot through, and spoon over chops. Makes 4 servings.

Place meat on carving board and keep warm. Spoon fat from roast drippings; discard. Add water to drippings and heat to boiling; spoon into a sauce bowl to serve over roast slices. Garnish roast with lemon wedges to squeeze over each serving. Makes 8 to 10 servings.

Lamb Roll Provençal

Let your meatman roll the anchovies inside the roast after he bones it; be sure to have the anchovies there for him to use.

- 5-pound center-cut leg of lamb, boned
- 1 can (2 oz.) anchovy fillets, drained
- 3 cloves garlic
- ½ cup **dry Vermouth**
- ½ teaspoon salt
- About ¼ teaspoon freshly ground pepper
- 1 tablespoon olive oil
- 1 teaspoon whole oregano, crumbled
- ½ cup water
- 1 lemon, cut in wedges

Direct your meatman to distribute anchovies evenly over lamb then roll and tie for roasting. (Otherwise, unroll at home, place anchovies inside, then reroll and tie.) Cut garlic into slivers and insert them into the seams of the rolled, tied roast. Insert meat thermometer in the center and place in a roasting pan.

Mix together the Vermouth, salt, pepper, oil, and oregano for a basting sauce. Roast meat in a 325° oven, spooning wine sauce over it two or three times. Continue roasting until meat thermometer registers 140° for rare, 150° for medium, or 160° for medium-well done meat.

Ragout of Lamb

A rich brown gravy enhanced by white wine unites the meat and vegetable flavors in this braised lamb dish. Use a wine such as a Chablis or a Green Hungarian.

- 2 pounds lamb, cut in 2-inch cubes
- 2 tablespoons olive oil or salad oil
- 1 medium-sized onion, sliced
- 1 bunch *each* carrots and turnips, whole or cut in halves
- 1 can (10¾ oz.) brown gravy
- 1 cup **medium-dry white wine**
- 1 cup water
- 2 medium-sized tomatoes, peeled and sliced (or 2 tablespoons tomato paste)
- 2 cloves garlic, minced or mashed
- Salt and pepper to taste
- ¼ cup finely chopped parsley

In a large frying pan, sauté the lamb pieces in oil until well browned on all sides. Remove meat to a 2-quart casserole. In the same frying pan put the sliced onion, the carrots, and turnips; cook, stirring frequently, over medium heat, until well browned. Put the carrots and turnips into the casserole with the meat. Drain off the fat from frying pan, leaving onions in; add the brown gravy, wine, water, tomatoes, and garlic, and simmer 20 to 30 minutes. Put through a food mill or strainer; add salt, pepper, and parsley; pour over meat and vegetables in casserole. Cover casserole and put into a 375° oven and bake 1 hour until tender. Makes about 6 servings.

Lamb and Sausage Soup

Lamb, ham, sausage, vegetables, and wine make this soup a full meal in one bowl. A little wine is added to each serving; present in a small decanter, if you like, to pass. Use a wine such as a Chianti or a Barbera.

1 package (12 oz.) dried lentils
2 medium-sized carrots, coarsely diced
3 medium-sized onions, chopped
9 cups water
About 1½ teaspoons salt
4 lamb shanks
¾ pound ham hock
1 cup **dry red wine**
6 to 8 garlic sausages
About ½ cup **dry red wine**

Wash lentils in cold water and drain well; place in a large kettle. Add carrots, onions, water, and salt to the lentils. Bring the mixture to a boil and add lamb shanks, ham hock, and the 1 cup wine. Cover and simmer gently for about 2½ hours or until meats are very tender. If you wish, remove bones and fat from meats and discard; skim excess fat from surface of soup.

Add the garlic sausages, whole or cut in thick slices, and simmer soup for about 20 minutes more. Ladle soup into large serving bowls and add about 1 tablespoon wine to each bowl. Makes 6 to 8 servings.

Indian Lamb Curry

Use a wine such as a Burgundy or a Gamay in this curry-flavored lamb and apple stew.

2 tablespoons butter or bacon drippings
2 pounds boneless lamb, cut in cubes
4 medium-sized onions
3 large tart apples such as Newtown Pippins
2 cloves garlic, minced
2 tablespoons *each* all-purpose flour and curry powder
1½ teaspoons ground ginger
1 teaspoon salt
1 cup *each* canned condensed consommé and **dry red wine**
1 teaspoon lemon juice
3 cups hot cooked rice
Assorted condiments: raisins, chopped salted peanuts, Major Grey's chutney, minced green onion, diced banana

Melt butter in a large heavy pan; add meat and brown, turning to brown all sides. Peel and slice onions and add to the pan; sauté until golden. Peel and slice apples and sauté until slightly limp. Add garlic, then sprinkle with flour, curry powder, ginger, and salt, blending. Stir in consommé, wine, and lemon juice. Simmer slowly for 2 hours, or until meat is tender and flavors are blended. Serve on a mound of rice. Accompany with condiments in small, separate bowls to spoon onto individual servings. Makes 4 to 6 servings.

Lamb Parmesan

1 boned leg of lamb (about 5 lbs.)
⅓ cup all-purpose flour
⅓ cup olive oil
2 cloves garlic, crushed
1 can (10½ oz.) condensed mushroom soup
1 can (8 oz.) tomato sauce
2 cups **Marsala**
2 tablespoons sour cream
1 onion, thinly sliced
1 cup fresh medium-sized mushrooms, whole
1 tablespoon chicken stock base or 2 chicken bouillon cubes
2 teaspoons salt
¾ teaspoon pepper
½ teaspoon marjoram
About ½ cup shredded Parmesan cheese
Hot cooked rice

Trim off fat and discard from meat; cut lamb into ¼-inch slices. Coat lightly with flour; shake off excess. In a frying pan brown slices without crowding in olive oil with 1 of the cloves of garlic. Place as browned in large casserole. Blend remaining garlic clove, soup, tomato sauce, Marsala, sour cream, onion, mushrooms, stock base, salt, and pepper and pour over lamb. Sprinkle with cheese and bake in a 350° oven 1 hour, stirring twice. Serve over rice. Makes 6 to 8 servings.

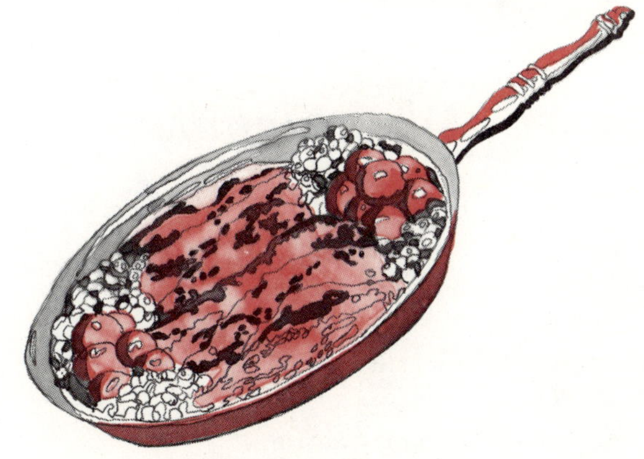

POULTRY WITH A TOUCH OF THE GRAPE

Improving on Chicken and Turkey

The chicken dishes in this chapter have predominantly international inspiration drawing from the cuisine of the Basque, the Japanese, the Italian, and the French. Some are simple sautés, others baste while roasting. Some have a delicious sauce. Wine contributes to each.

Complete instructions for roast turkey with a delightful herbed rice stuffing and brown giblet gravy are given in the section on turkey. Also included are recipes just for turkey breasts and legs for those with preferences.

Roast Chicken Flambé

- 4 to 5-pound roasting chicken
- Salt
- ½ cup (¼ lb.) unsalted butter
- 1 stalk celery
- ¾ cup **brandy,** warmed
- ½ cup **Port**
- 2 tablespoons whipping cream
- Pepper
- French bread, sliced

Rub chicken inside and out with salt, and place butter and celery in the cavity. Set chicken on a rack in a baking pan and brown in a 425° oven for 15 minutes. Remove from oven, pour over warm brandy, and ignite, basting chicken until flame dies. Drench with Port and cream; sprinkle with pepper, and add more salt, if needed. Bake in a 325° oven, basting continually, until chicken is a deep brown and cooked through (the leg joint will move easily). Tilt chicken to drain cavity juices into pan. Transfer to a board to carve and serve on French bread slices; spoon over the pan juices. Makes 4 to 6 servings.

Chicken Breasts Veronique

The use of *veronique* in the title of a dish usually indicates that wine and grapes are major elements and French cuisine is the influence. Use a wine such as a dry Sauterne or a dry Semillon.

- 4 whole chicken breasts (about 1 lb. *each*), halved, boned, and skinned
- Salt
- 2 tablespoons butter
- 1½ tablespoons orange marmalade
- ½ teaspoon tarragon
- ½ cup *each* **dry white wine** and whipping cream
- 2 teaspoons cornstarch
- Water
- 1½ cups Thompson seedless grapes

Sprinkle chicken breasts lightly with salt. Melt butter in a wide frying pan over medium heat. Add breasts; brown lightly on each side.

Blend with chicken the marmalade, tarragon, and wine. Cover pan and simmer very gently for about 20 minutes, or until thickest section of breast is white through. Transfer breasts to a serving dish and keep hot.

To pan juices add the whipping cream and quickly bring to a rolling boil. Blend the cornstarch with a little water and stir into sauce; return to boil, stirring. Add the grapes, return to boil, then immediately pour sauce over chicken. Makes 4 servings.

Basque Chicken

Braised chicken, Basque-style, cooks with vegetables and Canadian bacon. Use a wine such as Chablis or Mountain White.

- 1 large broiler-fryer chicken, about 3½ pounds
- Salt and pepper
- 1 tablespoon butter or margarine
- 2 tablespoons olive or salad oil
- ¼ pound Canadian bacon, diced
- ¼ pound medium-sized mushrooms, sliced
- 1 medium-sized onion, chopped
- 2 green peppers, seeded
- 2 tablespoons minced parsley
- 1 can (about 14½ oz.) pear-shaped tomatoes
- ½ cup **dry white wine**
- 2 large fresh tomatoes, peeled
- About 4 cups hot cooked rice
- 3 tablespoons water
- 4½ teaspoons cornstarch

Wash chicken and pat dry; sprinkle lightly inside and out with salt and pepper. Melt butter with 1 tablespoon of the oil in a Dutch oven over medium heat. Put in the whole chicken and sauté until golden, turning the bird to brown as evenly as possible on all sides. Remove to platter; set aside. Put in the Dutch oven the bacon; mushrooms; onion; 1 of the green peppers, chopped; and the parsley. Cook, stirring occasionally, for 15 minutes. Drain liquid from canned tomatoes into pan; crush the tomatoes, then add with the wine to the pan. Return chicken to pan, cover, reduce heat, and simmer until chicken is just done (leg moves easily when jiggled), about 45 minutes.

While chicken is simmering, cut fresh tomatoes in wedges, and slice remaining pepper into ¼-inch strips.

When chicken is done, remove from pan and place on bed of rice on a serving platter. Cover with foil and keep warm in a low oven.

Quickly return pan juices to boiling. Blend water smoothly with cornstarch and stir into juices; boil, stirring, until thickened. Pour into serving bowl; keep warm.

In a frying pan, heat the remaining tablespoon oil over medium-high heat. Add green pepper strips and cook, stirring, for 2 minutes; add fresh tomatoes and cook, stirring gently, for 2 more minutes or just until hot. Remove chicken from oven; arrange pepper and tomatoes around base. Carve chicken and serve sauce over meat, rice, and vegetables. Makes 4 servings.

Chicken Sauté, Mascotte

You can use whole chickens, cut up, or selected meaty parts in this recipe. Canned artichoke hearts can be substituted for fresh. Use a wine such as a Chablis or a Pinot Blanc.

- 2 broiler-fryer chickens (2½ to 3 lbs. *each* or 2 whole chicken breasts, and 4 *each* legs and thighs)
- Salt, pepper, and paprika
- 2 tablespoons *each* butter and olive oil
- ⅛ teaspoon *each* tarragon and rosemary
- ½ pound medium-sized mushrooms
- Juice of 1 lemon (about 3 tablespoons)
- ¾ cup **dry white wine**
- 2 tablespoons **dry Sherry**
- 2 teaspoons chicken stock base
- 6 small cooked artichokes, cut in halves, or 1 can (11 oz.) artichoke hearts, drained
- Finely chopped fresh parsley for garnish

Season chicken pieces with salt, pepper, and paprika. Using a large frying pan, brown chicken in butter and oil, turning to brown all sides. Sprinkle with tarragon and rosemary. Cover and let cook over medium heat for 35 to 40 minutes, or until tender. Remove chicken to a platter and keep it warm.

Quarter mushrooms and add to the pan with the lemon juice, white wine, Sherry, and stock base; simmer 3 to 4 minutes. Add artichokes to the pan juices and heat through. Spoon vegetables from the sauce over the chicken pieces. Quickly boil down sauce in pan until smooth and thickened, then spoon over chicken. Sprinkle with parsley. Makes 8 servings.

Chicken-Ham Marsala

- 6 large chicken thighs, boned
- ¼ pound boneless cooked ham, finely chopped or ground
- 2 tablespoons butter or margarine
- ½ cup sliced mushrooms
- 1 can (10½ oz.) condensed mushroom soup
- 1 cup sour cream
- ½ cup **Marsala**
- Paprika
- Cornstarch and water paste (optional)
- Hot cooked rice or split, buttered, toasted English muffins

Fill inside of chicken thighs with ham, fold over to close, and tie skin side out with string or secure with skewers.

Melt butter in a 9-inch-square baking pan. Turn chicken rolls over in butter to coat completely and place side by side.

Combine mushrooms, soup, sour cream, and wine and heat, stirring, just to boiling. Then pour mixture over chicken. Sprinkle well with paprika.

Bake, uncovered, in a 450° oven for 15 minutes. Cover; reduce heat to 350°, and bake 30 minutes, or until chicken is very tender when pierced.

If thicker gravy is desired, pour pan juices into a saucepan. Bring to boil and thicken, as desired, with cornstarch-water paste; pour back over chicken. Serve with rice or on muffins. Makes 3 servings of 2 thighs each.

Barbecued Sweet-Sour Chicken

This meat is first simmered in the sauce, then allowed to stand in it to absorb more flavor. Finally it is richly browned on a barbecue. Use a wine such as a Chablis or a dry Sauterne.

- 4 *each* chicken legs and thighs or 1 broiler-fryer chicken (2½ to 3 lbs.), cut up
- ⅓ cup *each* lemon juice and honey
- ½ cup **dry white wine**
- 2 tablespoons Worcestershire
- 3 tablespoons Dijon-style mustard
- ½ teaspoon salt
- ¼ teaspoon *each* basil and liquid hot pepper seasoning

Rinse chicken pieces and pat dry. In a Dutch oven combine the lemon juice, honey, wine, Worcestershire, mustard, salt, basil, and liquid hot pepper seasoning. Bring to boiling, put in chicken pieces, reduce heat, cover, and simmer gently until chicken is almost tender, about 35 minutes. Remove from heat and let stand for at least 30 minutes, or up to 3 hours.

To barbecue, lift chicken from marinade and arrange on the grill 4 to 6 inches over low, glowing coals. Watch carefully and turn often until browned and heated through, basting with the marinade. Makes about 4 servings.

Chicken Saltimbocca

Boned chicken breasts replace the veal in this innovation of Italy's *saltimbocca.*

- 6 whole chicken breasts (*each* about 1 lb.), split
- 12 paper-thin slices prosciutto (Italian-style ham) or boiled ham
- ¼ pound Swiss cheese, thinly sliced
- ¼ cup all-purpose flour
- 1 egg, slightly beaten
- ¼ cup fine dry bread crumbs
- 2 tablespoons shredded Parmesan cheese
- ¼ teaspoon *each* garlic salt and tarragon
- 4 tablespoons butter or margarine
- ½ cup regular-strength chicken broth
- ½ cup **dry Sherry**
- 1 tablespoon cornstarch blended with 1 tablespoon water

Bone chicken breasts and remove skin. Place a slice of ham and a thin slice of cheese on the underside of each chicken breast and roll up lengthwise. Skewer to hold with a toothpick. Dip chicken rolls in flour to coat, shake off excess, then dip in beaten egg, drain briefly, and roll in crumbs mixed with the Parmesan cheese, garlic salt, and tarragon. Brown chicken rolls in butter in a large frying pan, turning to brown all sides. Transfer to a baking dish and pour in chicken broth and Sherry. (It can be prepared ahead to this point and refrigerated.)

Bake, uncovered, in a 350° oven for 30 minutes (40 minutes if refrigerated), or until meat is white at center. Lift chicken out onto a serving platter and keep warm. Drain juices into a small saucepan, bring quickly to a boil, and blend in paste of cornstarch and water; stirring constantly, cook until thickened. Spoon sauce over chicken rolls. Makes 8 servings.

Yakitori

Yakitori indicates Japanese skewer cooking—broiled (yaki) chicken (tori). The chicken is basted with a Sherry and soy sauce combination and served with steamed rice.

- 2½ pounds chicken breasts (about 3 large whole breasts)
- 6 to 8 green onions
- ⅓ cup **dry Sherry**
- 2 tablespoons soy sauce
- ½ teaspoon shredded fresh ginger root (or ¼ teaspoon powdered ginger)
- 1 clove garlic, minced

Skin, bone, and split breasts. Cut each half breast into 4 pieces, making 1-inch-wide strips. Cut the white part only of the onions into 1¼-inch-long pieces. Alternate chicken and onion on each of 6 skewers, using all.

Mix together Sherry, soy sauce, ginger root, and garlic. Brush chicken with this sauce and grill about 4 inches over medium-hot coals (or broil 4 inches from the heat source), turning once, and basting with sauce. Cook until chicken is no longer pink inside, about 8 to 10 minutes. Makes 6 skewers; allow 1 or 2 for a serving.

Curry-Honey Chicken

Serve this curry-honey chicken and onions over hot steamed rice. Use a wine such as a Rhine or a White Riesling.

- 1 broiler-fryer chicken (about 3 lbs.), quartered
- 1 teaspoon salt
- ¾ teaspoon ground ginger
- ½ teaspoon pepper
- 1 medium-sized onion, thinly sliced
- 2 tablespoons soft butter or margarine
- ¾ cup **dry white wine**
- 4 tablespoons honey
- 1 tablespoon curry powder

Rinse chicken quarters; dry each section well. Combine salt, ginger, and pepper, and rub over the chicken sections. Place onion slices in the bottom of a well greased, 9 by 13-inch baking pan. Put chicken on onions, skin side up; dot with butter. Pour wine over top; bake in a 400° oven about 50 minutes. During the last 20 minutes, baste several times with a mixture of honey and curry. Makes 4 servings.

Chicken Cacciatore à la Romano

Chicken, simmered in a rich red sauce, is served the traditional way—over hot spaghetti. Use Chablis or dry Vermouth.

- 2½ to 3-pound broiler-fryer chicken, cut up
- All-purpose flour
- 3 tablespoons olive oil
- 3 tablespoons butter or margarine
- 1 medium-sized onion, chopped
- ½ pound small mushrooms, sliced; or 1 can (6 or 8 oz.) whole button mushrooms, drained
- 2 teaspoons chopped parsley
- 1 clove garlic, minced or mashed
- 1 cup **dry white wine**
- 1 can (10¾ oz.) spaghetti sauce with mushrooms
- 2 bay leaves
- ½ teaspoon salt
- ⅛ teaspoon pepper
- 4 ounces spaghetti
- Boiling salted water
- 2 tablespoons warm olive oil

Dredge chicken pieces in flour to coat and shake off excess; sauté in the 3 tablespoons olive oil in a heavy frying pan until browned on all sides. Remove chicken from pan and set aside. Add butter to the pan and sauté the onion and mushrooms until lightly browned. Add parsley, garlic, and wine; stir to scrape browned bits from bottom of pan. Return chicken to pan; cover and simmer 10 minutes. Add spaghetti sauce, bay leaves, salt, and pepper. Cover and simmer for 35 minutes, or until tender. Remove bay leaves.

Meanwhile cook spaghetti in a generous quantity of boiling salted water until just tender; drain, and stir in the 2 tablespoons warm olive oil. Spoon chicken and sauce over the top. Makes about 4 servings.

Baked Chicken with Apple

A combination of white wine, ginger, and apples blend smoothly with the chicken. Use a wine such as a Rhine or a Gewürztraminer, or even an apple wine.

- 1 teaspoon salt
- ¼ teaspoon pepper
- ⅛ teaspoon garlic powder
- ½ cup all-purpose flour
- 3 to 3½-pound broiler-fryer chicken, cut up
- 2 tablespoons *each* butter and salad oil
- 3 firm cooking apples, peeled, cored, and quartered
- 2 tablespoons sugar
- 2 tablespoons finely chopped preserved or crystallized ginger
- 1½ cups **dry white wine**
- ½ cup plus 3 tablespoons water

Combine salt, pepper, garlic powder, and flour. Coat chicken pieces in flour mixture, shake off excess, and reserve extra seasoned flour. In a large frying pan, heat butter and oil over medium heat; brown chicken pieces, a few at a time, and transfer to a shallow 2½ quart casserole. Add apple quarters to frying pan, sprinkle with sugar, and brown lightly. Arrange apple pieces around chicken in casserole; sprinkle with ginger. This can be covered and refrigerated at this point.

Just before baking, add wine and the ½ cup water to the casserole. Cover and bake in a 350° oven for 45 minutes (1 hour if chilled) or until chicken is tender when pierced. Remove chicken and apple to warm serving dish; keep warm. Blend reserved flour mixture to a smooth paste with the 3 tablespoons water.

Pour casserole liquid into a saucepan, stir in flour paste, and quickly bring to a boil, stirring, until sauce is bubbly and thickened. If desired, pour sauce through a wire strainer, to remove bits of ginger. Spoon some of the sauce over chicken before serving. Pass remaining sauce. Makes 4 servings.

Chicken, Dijon Style

The Dijon area of France adjoins the Burgundy wine region making the pairing of the local products a natural occurrence. Chicken does well in a Dijon mustard and white wine sauce. Use a wine such as a Chablis or a Chardonnay.

- 2 broiler-fryer chickens, cut up
- 2 tablespoons salad oil
- 1 teaspoon salt
- ¼ teaspoon *each* pepper and thyme
- ½ teaspoon tarragon
- ⅛ teaspoon cayenne
- 1 bay leaf
- 1 cup **dry white wine**
- ½ cup regular-strength chicken broth
- 3 egg yolks
- 2 tablespoons Dijon-style mustard
- ¼ cup sour cream

Dry chicken thoroughly and heat salad oil in a large frying pan. Brown chicken, a few pieces at a time, in hot oil over high heat. Return all pieces to pan and sprinkle with salt, pepper, thyme, tarragon, and cayenne; add the bay leaf and pour in wine and broth. Cover and let simmer gently about 45 minutes, or until chicken is just tender. Remove chicken to a warm platter and keep warm.

Beat egg yolks and mustard together and gradually stir in 2 or 3 tablespoons of the hot cooking liquid, stirring to blend thoroughly. Return yolks and sauce to pan and cook, stirring, over low heat just until liquid is slightly thickened. Remove from heat and blend in sour cream. Pour sauce through a wire strainer over chicken. Makes 6 to 8 servings.

Herb Barbecued Chicken

- 3 cups olive oil
- 2 cups **dry white wine**
- ½ cup wine vinegar
- 2 teaspoons salt
- ½ teaspoon *each* dry mustard and pepper
- 3 bay leaves
- 1 tablespoon crumbled rosemary
- 1½ teaspoons crumbled basil
- 2¼ teaspoons crumbled oregano
- Dash *each* cayenne and liquid smoke seasoning
- ½ cup chopped parsley
- 3 medium-sized cloves garlic, pressed
- 2 broiler-fryer chickens (about 3 lbs. *each*), quartered

Combine oil, wine, vinegar, salt, mustard, pepper, bay leaf, rosemary, basil, oregano, cayenne, liquid smoke, parsley, and garlic in a large bowl; let stand 2 hours or longer. Immerse chicken in sauce, then place 8 to 10 inches above well-ignited charcoal on grill. Cook 45 minutes to 1 hour or until meat pulls easily from thigh and breast is white through.

Turn frequently and brush generously with sauce. Makes 8 servings.

Coq au Vin with Olives

Coq au Vin or chicken with wine is aptly named; here it is prepared in quantity using three chickens and a bottle of Burgundy or Gamay.

- ½ cup butter or margarine
- 3 large broiler-fryer chickens (about 3 lbs. *each*), cut up
- ¼ cup **brandy**
- 1 bottle (⅘ qt.) **dry red wine**
- 1 tablespoon salt
- ¼ teaspoon nutmeg
- ½ teaspoon crumbled rosemary
- 1 bay leaf
- 1 tablespoon chicken stock base
- 3 cloves garlic, minced or mashed
- 1½ pounds mushrooms (caps *each* 1-inch diameter)
- 1½ tablespoons lemon juice
- 4 slices extra-thick sliced bacon, finely diced
- 2 cans (about 1 lb. *each*) small whole onions
- 2 teaspoons sugar
- ⅓ cup *each* cornstarch and water
- 1 jar (7 oz.) pimiento-stuffed olives

Melt 2 tablespoons of the butter in each of 2 large frying pans; cook chicken pieces, turning to brown all sides. Warm brandy, ignite, and pour flaming over the chicken; spoon sauce over chicken until flame dies. Add wine and stir to free the browned drippings, then transfer chicken and liquid to an 8-quart kettle or Dutch oven with a cover. Add salt, nutmeg, rosemary, bay, chicken stock base, and garlic. Cover and simmer gently for 1 hour, or until chicken is barely tender. Remove from heat.

Meanwhile, slice stems from mushrooms and leave caps whole; in one of the frying pans, sauté stems and caps in the remaining ¼ cup butter along with lemon juice until limp; transfer mushrooms and juices to the chicken.

Using the same pan, sauté the bacon until crisp; remove from pan and drain on paper towels. Pour off all but 2 tablespoons bacon drippings and add well-drained onions to the pan. Sprinkle with sugar and heat, shaking pan until onions are lightly browned. Add onions to chicken.

Blend cornstarch with water to make a paste. Drain wine juices from the chicken into a saucepan and heat to boiling; stir in cornstarch and heat until thickened, stirring constantly. Pour back over chicken in casserole. Add drained olives and sprinkle with crisped bacon. (The dish can be refrigerated at this point.)

Cover and place in a 350° oven to heat thoroughly; about 20 minutes. (Bake 1 hour and 15 minutes if refrigerated.) Makes 8 to 10 servings.

Drumstick Dumplings

Wrap boned chicken legs in refrigerated biscuits and bake in a wine flavored gravy.

- 2 packages (1 lb. *each*) frozen chicken legs or thighs, thawed
- 1 tablespoon butter or margarine
- 1½ cups regular-strength chicken broth
- ½ teaspoon celery salt
- Salt
- 2 tablespoons cornstarch
- ½ cup **dry Vermouth**
- 2 packages (8 oz. *each*) refrigerator biscuits
- 1 tablespoon half-and-half or milk

Using a large frying pan with cover, cook chicken pieces in melted butter, turning to brown all sides. Pour in chicken broth, add celery salt and salt to taste. Cover and simmer slowly until tender, about 30 minutes. Remove chicken from stock and let cool until cool enough to handle. Then remove skin and bones, leaving each leg or thigh whole.

Meanwhile blend cornstarch and wine and stir into the hot chicken broth; cook, stirring, until thickened. Pour gravy into a 9 by 13-inch baking pan or dish. Roll out refrigerated biscuits to make each a 3-inch circle. Wrap one dough circle around each piece of chicken, press edges together to seal, and place in the baking pan. Brush the tops of the biscuit dumplings with half-and-half. Bake in a 400° oven for 20 minutes or until lightly browned. Arrange dumplings on a platter and serve gravy in a sauce bowl. Makes 6 to 8 servings.

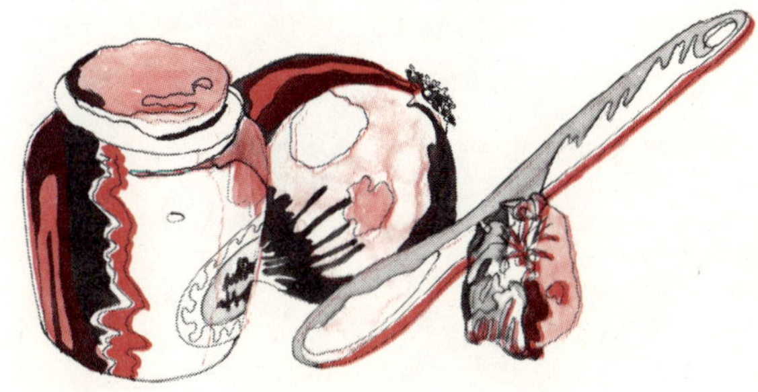

Turkey

Roast Turkey

This turkey recipe calls for four forms of wine in its preparation: Brandy and Port baste the turkey, enriching its flavor and color; the herbed rice stuffing includes Sherry; and the brown giblet gravy uses dry Vermouth.

- 12 to 16-pound turkey
- Herbed rice stuffing (recipe follows)
- About ½ cup (¼ lb.) melted butter or margarine
- ½ cup warm **brandy**
- ⅔ cup **Tawny Port**
- Brown giblet gravy (recipe follows)

Wash turkey well and pat dry inside and out. Fill neck cavity with rice stuffing and close it with skewers; fasten wings to body with skewers. Turn over and fill body cavity. Leave legs free for best heat penetration.

Put turkey, breast down, on a rack in a shallow pan. Insert meat thermometer into thickest part of the breast meat. Brush turkey with some of the melted butter and put into a 325° oven.

The turkey is done when thermometer registers 175°. Total cooking time for this size turkey is about 3 to 3¾ hours. Baste with melted butter or pan drippings every half hour.

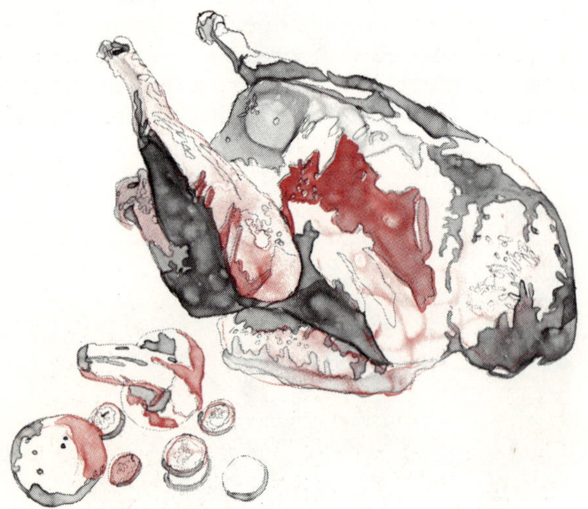

When turkey is almost done (170°), remove from oven; working quickly using pot holders and paper towels, lift turkey from the rack onto a waiting baking sheet. Pour all the drippings from the roasting pan into a bowl or pan; reserve for sauce. Turn turkey breast up and replace on rack in roasting pan.

Warm brandy in a small pan; ignite and pour flaming over the turkey; keep spooning it over bird until flames die. Then quickly heat Port and 2 tablespoons of the butter in the same pan and slowly pour over turkey, making sure it completely coats the bird. Put back in oven until nicely browned—about 20 minutes. Then put on platter, cover with foil, and let rest for 20 to 30 minutes before carving. Add all additional drippings for gravy. Makes about 12 servings, plus leftovers.

Herbed Rice Stuffing:

- 1½ cups regular long grain rice
- 3 cups regular-strength chicken broth
- 6 tablespoons butter or margarine
- 2 medium-sized onions, chopped
- 1 large carrot, shredded
- 4 stalks celery, sliced
- 1 clove garlic, minced or mashed
- ¼ cup minced parsley
- ¼ pound mushrooms, sliced
- 1½ teaspoons *each* poultry seasoning and grated lemon peel
- ¼ teaspoon *each* pepper and thyme
- 1 teaspoon salt
- ⅓ cup **dry Sherry**
- ⅔ cup sliced almonds or coarsely chopped filberts

Add rice to boiling chicken broth, stir, reduce heat to low, cover, and cook 20 minutes until liquid is absorbed. Meanwhile melt butter in a large frying pan; add onion and sauté until limp. Add carrot, celery, garlic, parsley, and mushrooms; sauté until liquid from vegetables has evaporated. Stir in poultry seasoning, lemon peel, pepper, thyme, and salt. Combine the vegetables with rice. Add Sherry and nuts and mix lightly. Makes about 4 cups stuffing, or enough for a 12 to 16-pound turkey.

Brown Giblet Gravy:

- 4 tablespoons butter or margarine
- Turkey giblets
- 2 carrots, finely chopped
- 1 onion, finely chopped
- ½ cup finely chopped parsley
- ¼ cup **dry Vermouth**
- 6 cups regular-strength chicken broth
- Fat-free juices from roast turkey
- 4 to 6 tablespoons cornstarch blended with 6 tablespoons water

Melt butter in a saucepan and add liver; cook just until firm and set aside. To butter add thinly sliced heart and gizzard, the carrots, onion, and parsley. Cook on high heat, stirring until mixture is very well browned. Pour in Vermouth and boil until evaporated. Add turkey neck and chicken broth to saucepan. Cover and simmer gently for 1½ hours.

Pour broth through a wire strainer and discard all but the liquid. Return broth to saucepan and add turkey juices. Bring to a rolling boil, stirring in as much of the cornstarch paste as needed to thicken to desired consistency. Chop liver and add to gravy; serve hot. Makes about 6 cups.

Turkey Tarragon Scallopini

Turkey breast, sliced and pounded thin, is cooked quickly in butter and flavored with dry Vermouth and tarragon. If you pound the breast ahead, the dish can be quickly cooked just before serving.

- About 1½ pounds boneless uncooked turkey breast
- ¼ cup all-purpose flour
- About 5 tablespoons butter or margarine
- ¼ pound mushrooms, sliced
- 1 tablespoon finely chopped parsley
- ¼ teaspoon *each* salt and tarragon
- ⅛ teaspoon pepper
- ⅓ cup **dry Vermouth**

Cut turkey across the grain into ½-inch-thick slices; lay slices between waxed paper and pound with a flat surfaced meat mallet until slices are uniformly ¼ inch thick. Pound evenly and gently to avoid tearing meat, replacing paper as needed. Dredge pieces of meat in flour, coating all over; shake off excess flour.

Melt half the butter in a large frying pan over medium-high heat; add turkey slices without crowding and cook until just lightly browned on each side; takes about 4 minutes total. Transfer cooked pieces to a serving dish and cover to keep warm.

Melt remaining butter in pan, reduce heat to medium, add mushrooms, and cook until they are limp, about 5 minutes. Stir in parsley, salt, tarragon, pepper, and Vermouth; boil for about 2 minutes stirring to incorporate brown bits clinging to pan. Pour evenly over turkey and serve. Makes 4 to 6 servings.

Braised Turkey Drumsticks

Use all drumsticks or a combination of drumsticks and thighs; the sauce is good on split baked potatoes. Use a wine such as a Chablis or a Mountain White.

- 4 turkey legs, or 2 *each* legs and thighs (3 to 3½ lbs. *each*)
- ¼ cup butter or margarine
- 1 clove garlic, minced or mashed
- 1 large onion, sliced and separated into rings
- 1½ cups *each* diagonally sliced celery and carrots
- ½ cup *each* regular-strength chicken broth and **dry white wine**
- 1 teaspoon seasoned salt
- ⅛ teaspoon pepper
- 1 tablespoon all-purpose flour

Brown turkey in butter in a large frying pan. Add garlic, onion, celery, and carrots, and sauté until onions are soft. Stir in chicken broth, wine, seasoned salt, and pepper. Bring to a boil, reduce heat, cover, and simmer for about 2 hours or until turkey is very tender. Remove turkey and vegetables to a warm serving dish with a slotted spoon. Stir a little of the pan liquid into flour to make a smooth paste. Over high heat, quickly reduce sauce in pan by about ⅓; blend in flour mixture and cook, stirring constantly, until thickened. Pour over turkey. Makes 4 to 6 servings.

DOWN TO THE SEA WITH WINE

Fish and Shellfish

The delicate flavor of fish and shellfish is gracefully accented by wine. Dry white wine or dry Vermouth are reliable additions, and if handled judiciously, Sherry is complementary.

Cooking methods range from sautéing, broiling, baking to poaching. A classic representative of the soup-stew variety is the famous Cioppino from San Francisco's Fisherman's Wharf. When the influence is foreign the fish choices offered are domestic.

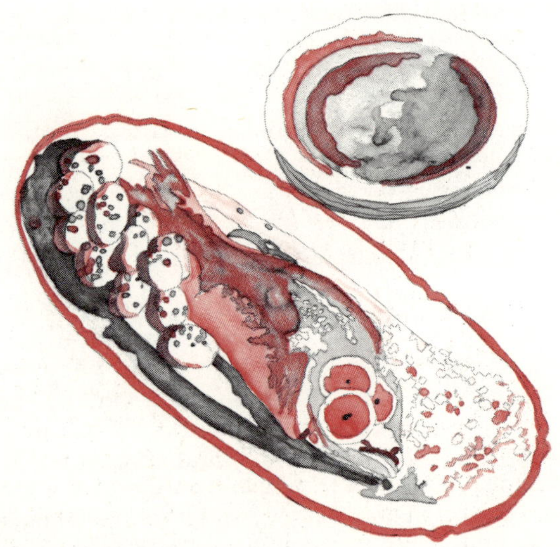

Barbecued Sablefish Teriyaki

The sablefish is also called the black cod or butter fish depending on what part of the country you are in. It is a rich fish like salmon but white with a mild flavor.

2 to 3 lb. piece sablefish, cut lengthwise into 2 fillets
¼ cup soy sauce
½ cup **dry Sherry**
2 tablespoons lemon juice
½ teaspoon fresh grated ginger (or ¼ teaspoon ground ginger)

Place fillets skin side down on pieces of heavy foil the size of the fish. In a pan combine the soy sauce, Sherry, lemon juice, and ginger; simmer 2 to 3 minutes to reduce slightly. Brush soy mixture on flesh sides of fish. Let stand about 30 minutes. Place fish, with foil sides down, on grill about 6 inches over medium-hot coals. Cover grill with a lid or hood of foil to enclose fish on grill. Baste several times with soy mixture, until fish flakes when tested with a fork, about 15 minutes. Makes 4 to 6 servings.

Sole Paupiettes with Lemon Sauce

These delicately flavored sole paupiettes are filled with crab, and are served with a wine-lemon sauce. Use a wine such as a Chablis or a Chardonnay.

¾ pound cooked crab, finely chopped
1¼ cups fine bread crumbs
2 eggs, slightly beaten
¼ cup lemon juice
2 tablespoons minced parsley
½ teaspoon *fines herbes*
¼ teaspoon salt
Dash pepper
1½ pounds boneless fillet of sole
½ cup *each* **dry white wine** and regular-strength chicken broth
2 tablespoons *each* butter and all-purpose flour
Dash *each* salt and pepper
2 tablespoons lemon juice

To make filling, combine crab, crumbs, eggs, ¼ cup lemon juice, parsley, fines herbs, salt, and pepper. Stuff and roll fillets placing about 1 tablespoon filling on each fillet; fold the sides over the filling and roll the fish to enclose filling. Secure with short metal skewers or tie at each end with string. Place rolls in a large frying pan, add wine and broth, bring to a boil, and simmer about 10 minutes.

Meanwhile, melt butter in small pan and stir in flour, add salt and pepper. Cook 1 minute on medium heat, then remove from heat. Remove skewers or strings and arrange cooked fish rolls on a warm platter; keep warm. Strain cooking liquid from fish (there should be about ¾ cup; if not, add water to make this total) and gradually add to butter-flour mixture; cook, stirring until smooth and thickened. Stir in remaining 2 tablespoons lemon juice and pour sauce over fish paupiettes. Makes about 18 rolls and serves 6 to 8.

Sole Mousse with Shrimp

Cool cucumber slices and small shrimp decorate the top of this molded fish dish. Use a wine such as a Chablis or a dry Sauterne.

- 2 cups **dry white wine**
- 1 *each* carrot and onion, thinly sliced
- 2 sprigs parsley
- 1 teaspoon salt
- 8 to 10 whole black peppers
- 2½ pounds boneless sole fillets
- 2 envelopes unflavored gelatin
- 1 small onion, minced
- 3 tablespoons butter
- 2 tablespoons all-purpose flour
- 1½ cups half-and-half
- Salt
- Juice of 1 lemon
- 2 teaspoons prepared mustard
- 2 cups whipping cream
- 1 pound small, cooked, deveined shrimp
- 1 cucumber, thinly sliced

In a wide shallow pan, combine wine, sliced onion and carrot, parsley, salt, and black peppers. Cover, bring to a boil, and simmer about 5 minutes. Poach the fish fillets in this stock a few at a time; cook 2 to 3 minutes, or until fish flakes. Lift fillets from stock with slotted spatula and place together in a pan. When all are cooked, drain into the stock any juice from pan holding the fish. Strain stock and save—you should have 2 cups (if not, add water to make this total). Grind fish through fine blade of food chopper or blender, using some of the stock to make a smooth paste.

Cool ½ cup of the stock, add gelatin and set aside to soften. Meanwhile cook minced onion in butter until soft, but not browned. Stir in flour and blend in half-and-half. Cook, stirring, until thickened. Remove from heat, salt to taste, and stir in gelatin mixture until dissolved. Add fish, lemon juice, any remaining stock, and mustard. Chill until partially set; whip cream until stiff and fold in. Pour into a straight sided, flat bottomed, round or square 3-quart mold. Cover and chill overnight.

To serve, unmold on a platter, decorate with shrimp and cucumber slices. Spoon extra shrimp over each serving. Makes 12 to 14 servings.

Avocado Masked Salmon

Use ripe avocados to make a smooth green sauce to cover the oven poached salmon. It makes a handsome buffet entrée. Use a wine such as a Chablis or a Riesling.

- 1 whole 6 to 7 pound salmon without head and tail
- Salt
- 1 medium-sized onion, thinly sliced
- 2 cups **dry white wine**
- ½ lemon, thinly sliced
- 1 bay leaf
- 1 teaspoon *each* tarragon and salt
- 10 whole black peppers
- 2 to 3 quarts boiling water
- Avocado mask (recipe follows)

Sprinkle inside of salmon with salt. Wrap fish in cheesecloth and place flat in a large baking pan. Add onion, wine, lemon, bay leaf, tarragon, salt, and whole black peppers to the pan. Pour over enough boiling water to just cover fish. Bake in a 350° oven until thick portion of fish flakes when tested with fork, about 25 to 30 minutes. Holding fish with cheesecloth to support it, lift from liquid and drain on rack.

While still slightly warm, remove cheesecloth from fish. Pull off skin and remove fins carefully; place salmon on serving tray to chill. Just before serving, spread fish thickly with avocado mask and decorate with parsley and lemon slices. Makes 12 servings.

Avocado Mask:

With a rotary beater or blender, blend smooth 2 medium-sized peeled, pitted ripe avocados, 1 can (6 oz.) Hollandaise sauce, ½ teaspoon tarragon, and the 3 tablespoons lemon juice or 2 tablespoons lime juice. Use all on salmon.

Company Fish Casserole

The sole is in a creamy sauce and bakes with an attractive soufflé-like topping. Use a wine such as Chablis or a Pinot Blanc.

1½ pounds sole fillets
1 teaspoon *each* salt and dill weed
1 tablespoon chopped parsley
½ cup **dry white wine**
About ⅓ cup milk
3 tablespoons *each* butter and flour
5 eggs, separated
3 tablespoons freshly grated Parmesan cheese

Fit the fish into a greased baking dish (about 7 by 11 inches) and sprinkle with salt, dill, and parsley; pour in wine. Cover tightly with foil and bake in a 400° oven for 10 minutes. Drain off stock, leaving fish in dish. Measure stock and add milk to make 1 cup liquid. In a pan, heat butter, add flour, and cook until bubbly. Gradually stir in liquid and cook until thickened. Remove from heat and beat in egg yolks.

(Refrigerate fish and sauce, if made ahead; drain fish again to use.)

Shortly before serving, beat egg whites, then fold into sauce. Sprinkle 1 tablespoon of the cheese over fish and then spoon sauce over it. Sprinkle with remaining cheese. Bake, uncovered, in a 400° oven for 15 minutes (30 minutes if refrigerated). Makes 4 to 6 servings.

Halibut with Wine and Lemon

Mild halibut responds well to this method of cooking. The fish is first marinated in a lemon and white wine mixture, then browned in butter. The marinade becomes the base of the sauce served over the halibut. Use a wine such as Mountain White or Chablis.

6 halibut steaks or fillets (about 2 lbs.)
1 egg
4 tablespoons lemon juice
1¼ cups **dry white wine**
½ teaspoon salt
⅛ teaspoon pepper
4 tablespoons butter or margarine
1 tablespoon minced parsley

Arrange fish in a single layer close together in a shallow pan. Beat together egg, 3 tablespoons of the lemon juice, 1 cup of the wine, salt, and pepper and pour over the fish. Cover lightly and chill for about 1 hour. Lift fish from marinade, draining. Heat 2 tablespoons of the butter in a wide frying pan; add fish and brown on both sides. Place fish on a heated platter in a warm place. In pan, melt the remaining 2 tablespoons butter; add ¼ cup of the marinade, the remaining 1 tablespoon lemon juice, and ¼ cup wine. Bring to low simmer. Pour some of the sauce over the fish and pass the remainder to add to each serving. Sprinkle with minced parsley. Makes 6 servings.

Poached Seabass with Shrimp Sauce

A well-flavored bouillon is the first step in this recipe and it can be prepared well ahead of time. In the bouillon you poach the fish, then use it to cook the shrimp and make the sauce. Use a wine such as a Chablis or a dry Sauterne.

1 large onion, chopped
2 tablespoons butter
2 quarts water
1 large carrot, chopped
3 stalks celery, sliced
2 sprigs parsley
2 whole cloves
1 bay leaf
6 whole black peppers
2 teaspoons salt
2 tablespoons white vinegar
1 cup **dry white wine**
1 whole, washed seabass (or whole salmon) weighing 4 to 6 pounds

In a saucepan prepare the court bouillon by sautéing the onion in butter. Add water, carrot, celery, parsley, cloves, bay leaf, peppers, salt, vinegar, and wine. Simmer slowly for about 1 hour over low heat. Remove from heat, pour through a wire strainer, and discard vegetables and spices.

To cook the fish, bring court bouillon to a boil in a fish poaching pan (or improvise with a broiler pan or roasting pan) over direct heat. Lower fish into the boiling broth (wrap fish in cheesecloth if you don't have poaching pan with a rack). Cover pan and simmer either on top of the range or in a 400° oven for 7 to 10 minutes per pound or until fish flakes easily with a fork. When done, lift out of liquid and arrange fish (remove cheesecloth) on a warm serving plate. Cover with foil and put in a warm oven.

Shrimp Sauce:

½ pound medium-sized shrimp
6 tablespoons *each* butter and all-purpose flour
½ cup whipping cream
Salt
Garnish: fresh parsley, lemon slices, reserved whole shrimp

For the shrimp sauce, set the pan of court bouillon over high heat and boil rapidly, uncovered, until liquid is reduced by half, about 2½ cups. While broth is boiling, drop shrimp into it; cook 3 minutes, remove from broth, cool slightly, then peel and devein. Reserve a few shrimp for garnish; chop the remainder.

Meanwhile, melt the 6 tablespoons butter in another pan and stir in the flour. Cook until bubbly. Gradually stir in the reduced court bouillon and whipping cream. Cook until thickened; add chopped shrimp. Salt to taste.

Garnish fish plate with parsley and lemon. Decorate the fish with the whole shrimp. Pass hot shrimp sauce to spoon over each serving. Makes 8 to 10 servings.

Brazilian Baked Trout

Trout, baked in wine, works well with Chablis or a Rhine wine.

4 to 6 medium-sized trout (about ½ lb. *each*)
Juice of 1 lemon (3 tablespoons)
1 teaspoon salt
1 clove garlic, minced or mashed
1 cup **dry white wine**
2 tablespoons *each* chopped parsley, green onion, and dry bread crumbs
4 tablespoons melted butter

Wash and dry trout with paper towels; rub outside with lemon juice and sprinkle with salt. Arrange the minced garlic in the bottom of a buttered, shallow baking dish large enough to hold trout in a single layer. Place trout in dish; pour wine over top. Sprinkle the parsley, green onion, and dry bread crumbs over trout; then spoon butter evenly over all. Bake in a 400° oven for 20 minutes. Serve from baking dish. Makes 4 to 6 servings.

Fish in a Fish

There are many earthenware pots on the market shaped like fish for the purpose of baking fish. The important thing is to choose a container into which the fish fits snugly. Use a wine such as a Rhine or a Johannisberg Riesling.

3 pound tail portion of lingcod (or salmon)
1 small onion, finely chopped
2 cloves garlic, minced or mashed
2½ teaspoons salt
4 slices lemon
Water
¼ cup **dry white wine**
1 tablespoon lemon juice
¼ cup butter or margarine
2 teaspoons all-purpose flour

Cut belly of fish so it is open to within about 3 inches of tail. Combine onion, garlic, and 2 teaspoons of the salt; stuff into cavity of fish. Sprinkle remaining ½ teaspoon salt all over fish. Lay in a fish-shaped pot or tight-fitting pot and garnish with lemon slices.

Cover and bake in a 325° oven for 45 minutes to 1 hour, or until thickest portion of fish flakes with a fork.

Remove from oven. Holding lid ½ inch ajar, drain juices from pot, measure, and add water enough to make ¼ cup liquid; stir in wine and lemon juice; keep fish covered and warm. Heat butter in a small pan, stir in flour until smooth, gradually stir in cooking liquid; cook, stirring, until slightly thickened. Serve with the fish. Makes about 8 servings.

Shellfish

Shrimp Bordelaise

The classic French recipe calls for crayfish, but here shrimp substitute nicely. The vegetable *mire-poix* is the base of a rich sauce served over the shrimp. Use a wine such as a Chablis or a dry Sauterne.

1 large carrot, minced
1 medium-sized onion, minced
2 stalks celery, minced
¼ cup (⅛ lb.) butter
Pinch thyme
½ bay leaf
Salt and pepper to taste
2 pounds (about 30 to a lb.) large raw shrimp in shells
¼ cup **brandy**
2 cups **dry white wine**
3 egg yolks

Put carrot, onion, and celery in a heavy pan with butter, thyme, and bay leaf. Sauté, stirring, until vegetables are soft. Discard bay leaf and season with salt and pepper. Add wine.

Wash shrimp, cut shells down the back with scissors to remove sand veins. Loosen shells, but do not remove. Put unshelled shrimp in a pan. Warm brandy, ignite, and pour over shrimp. When flame dies, add to vegetables and wine. Cover and cook 10 minutes.

Remove shrimp with slotted spoon to rimmed platter and keep warm. Beat egg yolks with a little of the hot sauce in a cup; then stir into the sauce. Cook, stirring constantly, over low heat just until thick. Pour over shrimp. Makes 4 to 6 servings.

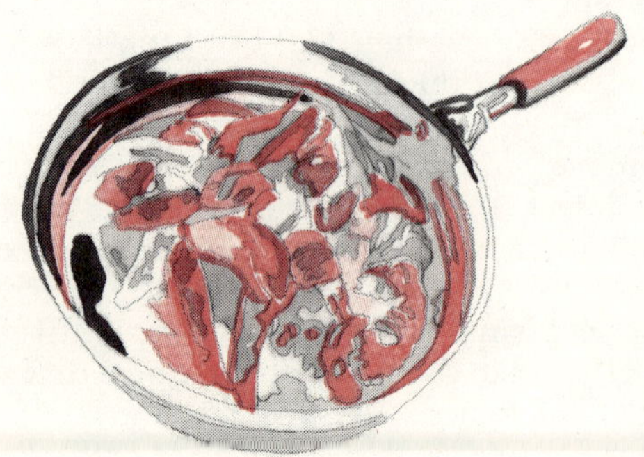

Lobster Imperial

This elegant entrée is cooked ahead to reheat at your convenience. Lobster tails flame with brandy then simmer in a tomato-wine sauce; you reheat them in the oven and finish with a broiled Hollandaise glaze. Use a wine such as a Chablis or a Chardonnay.

4 tablespoons butter
1 tablespoon salad oil
6 frozen rock lobster tails (about 8 oz. *each*) split and thawed
1 *each* medium-sized carrot and onion, finely chopped
2 cloves garlic, minced
½ teaspoon salt
⅓ cup **brandy**
4 tablespoons tomato paste
⅓ cup bottled clam juice
1½ cups **dry white wine**
½ teaspoon tarragon, crumbled
½ pound medium-sized mushrooms
1 tablespoon lemon juice
Hollandaise sauce (recipe follows)
Hot cooked white rice

Heat 2 tablespoons of the butter and 1 tablespoon salad oil in a large frying pan. Put in lobster tails, meat side down, the carrot and onion; sauté on high heat for 2 minutes. Add garlic and salt. Warm brandy, ignite, and spoon flaming over tails. Add tomato paste, clam juice, wine, and tarragon. Cover and simmer 5 to 6 minutes. Remove lobster tails from pan and let cool; loosen meat from shells. Chill until serving time.

Simmer sauce 10 minutes longer to blend flavors; then purée in a blender or push through a wire strainer. Slice mushrooms and sauté in the remaining 2 tablespoons butter with lemon juice; stir into the puréed tomato sauce. Chill.

To serve, place chilled lobster tails on a baking pan and heat in a 350° oven for 10 minutes. With a small spatula, spread a thick layer of Hollandaise sauce over the lobster meat. Slip under the broiler and broil 1 minute, or until brown. Serve on hot rice; accompany with sauce bowl of reheated mushroom sauce. Makes 6 servings.

Hollandaise:

Heat ¾ cup butter until melted and bubbly. In a blender place 3 egg yolks and 2 tablespoons lemon juice; blend a few seconds, then, with motor running, gradually pour in the hot butter in a slow steady stream. Blend just until the melted butter is incorporated into the sauce. Makes 1 cup. (Make this ahead of time and chill, if you wish, but let it warm to room temperature before using it.)

Wine-Baked Oysters

Have your local fish market open and shuck your oysters if you shy away from tackling this task. These are baked on the half shell with wine and seasoned crumbs. Use a wine such as a Chablis or a White Pinot.

- 1 dozen Eastern or small Pacific oysters in the shell (or 1 dozen shucked oysters and 12 half shells)
- Rock salt
- 1 cup cracker crumbs
- ¾ cup **dry white wine**
- About 4 tablespoons butter
- ¼ cup grated Parmesan cheese

Have oysters shucked at the fish market, reserving on one half shell for each or scrub oyster shells with vegetable brush under cold running water. Remove oysters from shells and drain in colander 10 to 15 minutes. Fill a large baking pan 1 inch deep with rock salt, and arrange oyster shells on it. Roll oysters in cracker crumbs, place one in each half shell, and add 1 tablespoon wine to each. Put about 1 teaspoon butter on top of each and sprinkle with Parmesan. Bake in a 350° oven for about 30 minutes. Transfer oysters to serving platter and serve hot. Makes 2 servings.

Steamed Clams in Wine Broth

Rock cockles, cherrystone, little-neck, bent-nose—all are names that mean "steamers" to clam lovers east and west. Accompany these wine-steamed clams with lemon or lime to squeeze over all and a small bowl of melted butter in which to dip the clams plucked from their shells. Sip the broth when you've finished the clams. Use a wine such as a Rhine or a Johannisberg Riesling.

- 3 pounds clams in the shell (about 6 clams per pound)
- ½ cup **dry white wine**
- 2 tablespoons butter
- ½ cup (¼ lb.) butter, melted
- 1 lime or lemon, cut in wedges

Scrub clams thoroughly with a brush in cold running water. Pour in wine into a kettle and add the 2 tablespoons butter and clams. Cover, bring to a boil, then reduce heat to simmer, cook until shells open, about 6 to 10 minutes. Arrange clams in their shells in shallow soup bowls and pour over the broth. Pour melted butter into individual serving bowls and garnish with lime or lemon wedges. Makes 4 to 6 first course servings or 2 main dish servings.

Shrimp Encino

This shrimp dish can be served from a chafing dish.

- 2½ pounds large uncooked fresh or frozen shrimp
- 6 tablespoons butter
- Salt
- 2 tablespoons lemon juice
- ¾ cup *each* **dry Vermouth** and water
- 1 bay leaf
- 1 medium-sized onion, sliced
- 6 whole black peppers
- 3 tablespoons all-purpose flour
- ½ cup whipping cream
- 5 tablespoons grated Romano cheese

Shell and devein raw shrimp. Melt 1 tablespoon of the butter in frying pan; lay shrimp in it, salt lightly, and sprinkle with lemon juice. Pour wine and water over; add bay leaf, onion, and peppers. Cover and simmer for 3 minutes; strain and reserve liquid. Set shrimp aside.

In frying pan, heat 3 more tablespoons of the butter, then slowly blend in flour; cook until bubbly. Gradually stir in cooking liquid and cook, stirring, until thickened. Taste and add more salt if needed.

Return shrimp to pan; cover and simmer about 3 minutes, or until shrimp are just bright pink and opaque in center (cut to test). Add remaining 2 tablespoons butter, quickly blend in cream, reheat, then remove from heat. If desired, pour shrimp and sauce into a heated chafing dish pan over hot water. Sprinkle with grated cheese and bring to the table to serve. Makes 4 servings.

Abalone in Wine

Whole abalone, brought home by the fisherman in the family, braised then simmered, is an unusual pot roasting technique for this shellfish. Wine and garlic enhance rather than hide the delicate abalone flavor. Use a wine such as a Chablis or a Riesling.

- 1 fresh whole abalone (about ¾ to 1 lb.)
- All-purpose flour
- Salt and pepper to taste
- 2 to 3 tablespoons olive oil
- 1 clove garlic, mashed
- 1 cup **dry white wine**
- ½ cup water
- Cornstarch blended to a paste with water (optional)

Pound abalone lightly with a wooden mallet until it feels limp all over. Dip in flour, shake off excess; sprinkle with salt and pepper. Brown over moderately-high heat on both sides in oil using a heavy pan with a tight-fitting cover. Add garlic, and the ½ cup water. Cover and simmer slowly for 40 minutes. Remove abalone from pan, keep warm. If desired, bring pan juices to boiling and thicken as desired with cornstarch paste. Serve to spoon onto portions of abalone. Slice abalone across grain thinly and serve. Makes 2 to 3 servings.

Broiled Scallops, Chinese

It only takes 5 minutes to broil these scallops after they marinate an hour or two. They can be served as hot appetizers or an entrée.

- 1½ pounds scallops
- ½ cup *each* salad oil or olive oil, soy sauce, and **dry Sherry**
- ½ teaspoon powdered ginger
- 1 clove garlic, minced or mashed

In a bowl large enough to hold the scallops, mix together the oil, soy sauce, and Sherry; stir in ginger and garlic. Wash and drain scallops and put into the soy mixture in the bowl, stirring until they are completely covered with the sauce; chill, covered, for 1 to 2 hours.

Just before serving, remove scallops from marinade and put on skewers, leaving a little space between scallops. Set on a broiler rack about 2 inches from the heat. Broil 4 to 5 minutes, turning several times, basting with marinade. Serve immediately. Makes 4 to 6 servings or 36 appetizers.

Shellfish Cioppino

A traditional favorite at San Francisco's Fisherman's Wharf is Cioppino (cho-*peen*-o). The purist prefers it prepared with all of the shellfish unshelled, as the flavors are better preserved and the dish is most inviting to look at; however it is easier to eat if the fish is shelled first. Serve with crusty French bread. Use red wine such as Chianti or Barbera; or white wine such as Chablis or a Chenin Blanc.

- 1 large onion, sliced
- 6 to 8 green onions, including part of the tops, sliced
- 1 green pepper, seeded and diced
- 2 whole large cloves garlic
- ⅓ cup olive oil or salad oil
- ⅓ cup chopped fresh parsley
- 1 can (1 lb.) tomato purée
- 1 can (8 oz.) tomato sauce
- 1 cup **dry red** or **dry white wine**
- 2 cups water (may be part wine)
- ½ bay leaf
- 1 tablespoon salt
- ¼ teaspoon pepper
- ⅛ teaspoon *each* whole dried rosemary and thyme
- 2 medium-sized Dungeness crabs (about 1½ lbs. *each*)
- 1 dozen clams in shells
- 1 pound prawns or large shrimp in shells

In a Dutch oven or a frying pan that has a cover, sauté the onion, green onion, green pepper, and garlic in olive oil about 5 minutes over medium-high heat. Add the parsley, tomato purée, tomato sauce, wine, water, bay, salt, pepper, rosemary, and thyme. Cover and simmer about an hour. Remove the garlic. (You can do this much ahead, if you wish, but reheat to use.)

Clean and crack the live Dungeness crabs, or have this done at your fish market just before you cook them; arrange crab in bottom of a large pan, at least 8-quart size. Scrub clams well under running water to remove sand and put in on top of crab. Cut shrimp or prawns down backs and wash out sand veins; put shrimp on top of clams. Pour on the hot prepared sauce, cover and simmer very gently until the clam shells open, 15 to 25 minutes.

Serve some of each shellfish and sauce in large soup bowls or soup plates. Have plenty of napkins handy. Makes about 6 servings.

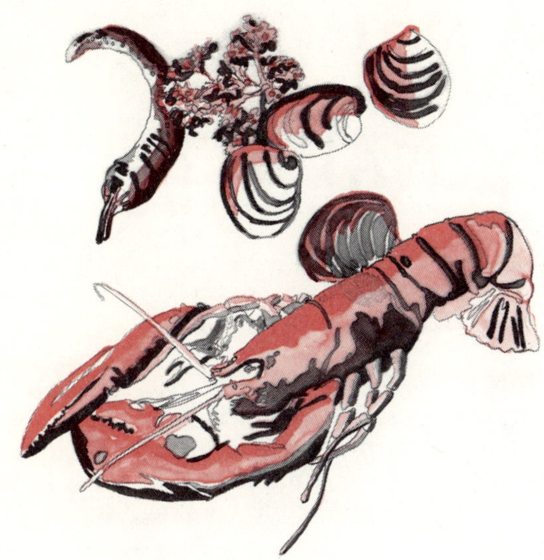

Seafood Bisque

This large-scaled main dish, creamy fish soup, is served with a selection of condiments, making it possible to individually style each serving. Use a wine such as a Riesling or a Traminer.

- 1¼ cups butter or margarine
- 1 cup instant-type all-purpose flour
- 4 cups fresh minced clams or 4 cans (7½ oz. *each*) minced clams
- 8 cups (½ gal.) milk
- 2 cups (1 pt.) half-and-half
- 6 to 8 green onions, including part of the tops, finely chopped
- 2 pounds crab meat
- 1 pound cooked and shelled small shrimp
- 1 cup **dry white wine**
- ⅓ cup **dry Sherry**
- Parsley sprig for garnish
- Assorted condiments: sieved hard-cooked egg yolks and egg whites (about 8 eggs), ¾ cup chopped chives, and ¾ cup chopped macadamia nuts

Melt ¾ cup of the butter in a 6-quart heavy-bottomed pan. Blend in flour and cook about 2 minutes over medium heat. Drain liquid from clams, reserve clams, and stir the liquid into butter until blended. Slowly stir in the milk and half-and-half; cook, stirring, until sauce is thickened.

Using a large frying pan, sauté onions in the remaining ½ cup butter, cooking until limp. Add the crab, shrimp, and drained clams, and cook in the butter until limp, stirring gently, until all the seafood is hot through. Add seafood to the soup; stir in wine and Sherry. Pour into a heated soup tureen or other large serving bowl. Garnish with parsley. Surround with small bowls of condiments. Makes 5 quarts or about 16 generous servings.

Cracked Crab in Wine Broth

Essential to the enjoyment of this dish is hot French bread spread with a pungent garlic butter to dunk into the broth. A whole bottle of dry white wine plus seasoning is the base in which you simply heat cooked Dungeness crab. Use a wine such as Chablis or a Folle Blanche.

- ¼ cup (⅛ lb.) butter or margarine
- 1 large onion, finely chopped
- 2 cloves garlic, minced or mashed
- ½ teaspoon liquid hot pepper seasoning
- ⅛ teaspoon cayenne
- ¼ cup chopped parsley
- 1 bay leaf
- 1 can (about 14 oz.) regular-strength chicken broth
- 1 bottle (⅘ qt.) **dry white wine**
- 2 large cooked Dungeness crabs (about 2 lbs. *each*), cleaned and cracked
- Lemon wedges
- Parmesan garlic bread (recipe follows)

In a large kettle (at least 8-qt.) heat butter until bubbly; stir in onion and garlic and cook over medium heat until onion is soft. Stir in hot pepper seasoning, cayenne, parsley, bay leaf, broth, and wine; heat to simmering. Add crab, cover, and simmer about 10 minutes or until crab is heated through.

Ladle crab and sauce into individual bowls; pass lemon wedges to squeeze over crab and hot Parmesan garlic bread to dunk in sauce. Makes 4 servings.

Parmesan Garlic Bread:

Mix ½ cup (¼ lb.) soft butter or margarine; 2 cloves garlic, minced or mashed; ¼ teaspoon paprika; and ¼ cup shredded Parmesan cheese. Cut 1 loaf (1 lb.) French bread to (but not through) bottom crust in 1-inch slices.

Generously spread butter mixture between bread slices; wrap loaf in heavy foil. To heat, put loaf in 325° oven for about 20 minutes.

WILD GAME AND VARIETY MEATS

Octopus, Frogs' Legs, Buffalo Meat

If you need a recipe for goat or octopus, buffalo or frogs' legs with a winey overtone, this is the chapter to find them in. Less adventurous perhaps, but equally interesting are preparation directions for wild and domestic pheasant and duck, and some for venison and rabbit. Each takes on new flavor delights with the addition of wine.

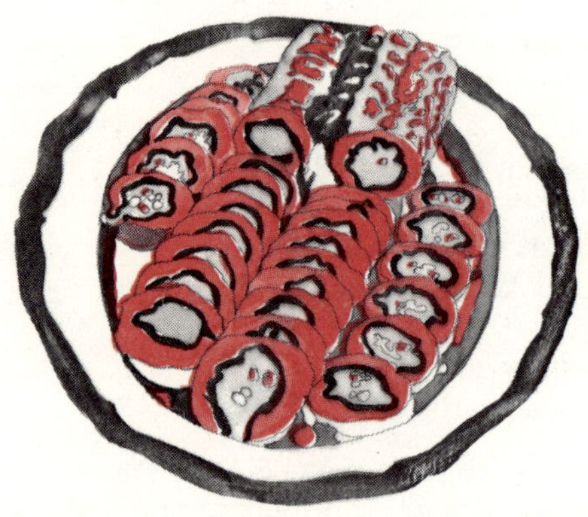

Band-Tailed Pigeon with Wine Sauce

This Western game bird takes well to the pronounced character of Tinta or Ruby Port, raisin, and clove sauce. Serve as a first course or a light entrée.

- 4 to 6 dressed band-tailed pigeons (about 7 to 10 oz. *each*), allow 2 birds per serving
- All-purpose flour
- 4 tablespoons butter
- About ¾ cup regular-strength beef broth
- ¼ cup **Tinta** or **Ruby Port**
- 2 to 3 tablespoons seedless raisins
- 2 whole cloves
- Canned or fresh grape leaves, optional. (To use fresh leaves: remove stems, immerse leaves in boiling water for 1 minute.)

Tie birds to hold legs against body. Coat each bird in flour, then dust off excess. Melt butter in a wide frying pan and brown birds on all sides taking care not to scorch butter. If necessary, tie birds so they will hold their shape while cooking. Remove ties before serving.

Add to the pan about half the broth, all the Port, raisins, and cloves. Cover and simmer for 30 minutes, adding remaining broth, a small portion at a time, to pan as juices evaporate.

Arrange birds on a platter or individual plates, remove strings, garnish with grape leaves (edible) and spoon on the sauce. Allow 1 bird for a first course serving or 2 to 3 birds for an entrée.

Roasted Game Hens with Orange Stuffing

These wine-glazed hens are split in half and oven-roasted with an orange-flavored stuffing.

- 2 frozen Rock Cornish game hens (about 20 to 24 oz. *each*)
- ½ teaspoon *each* salt and ground ginger
- ¼ teaspoon pepper
- ⅓ cup orange juice
- ¼ cup **dry Sherry**
- ½ teaspoon Worcestershire
- 1 teaspoon soy sauce
- Orange stuffing (recipe follows)
- 1 whole orange, sliced

Thaw hens according to package directions. Remove giblets and reserve for other uses. Wash hens well and pat dry. Cut hens in half using poultry shears. Season with salt, ginger, and pepper. Place in lightly greased broiler pan skin side down and roast in a 375° oven for 30 minutes. Mix together orange juice, Sherry, Worcestershire, and soy.

Turn over hen halves and brush with orange juice mixture.

Place orange stuffing in the pan alongside hens. Continue roasting 30 minutes longer, basting several times, until leg joint moves easily. Arrange halves on a platter with stuffing and garnish with orange slices. Makes about 4 servings.

Orange Stuffing:

Cut enough sliced sourdough French bread into small cubes to make 2¼ cups. Mix with ¼ cup orange juice, 1 teaspoon grated orange peel, 1 egg yolk, and 2 tablespoons finely chopped parsley.

Duckling with Raisin Sauce

First, brown the duckling on the barbecue, then seal the bird in foil with the seasonings and return to the barbecue to cook to moist succulence. Use a wine such as a dry Sauterne or a dry Semillon.

- 4½ to 5-pound duckling (thawed if frozen)
- 2 stalks celery, cut in chunks (include tops)
- 3 sprigs parsley
- ½ lemon, thinly sliced
- 4 teaspoons all-purpose flour
- ¼ teaspoon pepper
- 2 tablespoons soy sauce
- 2 cups **dry white wine**
- 1 bay leaf
- ¾ cup golden raisins

In a barbecue with a hood surround a foil drip pan (about the same size as the duck) on the fire bed with charcoal; ignite, and let coals burn until glowing. Wash duckling in cool water; dry with paper towels. Place celery, parsley, and lemon in duckling body cavity; fasten body and neck openings closed with wooden picks or skewers, and tie legs together.

Place duckling breast side up, on grill about 4 to 6 inches over foil drip pan; cover barbecue, adjust drafts, and cook for 1½ hours or until well browned. Remove duckling, and discard drip pan and fat; spread coals into center.

Center duckling on a double thickness of heavy foil to enclose it; turn sides up and add the remaining ingredients.Blend flour, pepper, and soy sauce; stir in wine. Pour wine mixture over duckling. Top with bay leaf and raisins. Enclose duckling in foil, sealing top and ends.

Return to covered barbecue, adding more charcoal as needed and cook over slow-burning coals for 1 hour longer.

Unwrap carefully and place duckling on warm platter; remove and discard stuffing. Pour raisin sauce from foil and serve separately to spoon over duckling. Makes 2 to 3 servings.

Carving:

A special technique is required to carve a duckling. First, cut off the thigh, including leg and wing, from one side; the thigh joint is further over and down on the back than on a chicken. Then starting at the collarbone, slip knife along the breastbone, removing the entire boneless half breast. Repeat on the other side. Slice boneless breast meat lengthwise. Disjoint thighs and drumsticks; discard carcass.

Pheasant Silverado

Pheasants raised in government controlled management areas intended for field trials are generally plump, well formed, and tender. Wild birds tend to be smaller, rangier, and tougher, and generally require more cooking per pound. Domestic pheasants were used in testing this recipe. Use a wine such as Chablis or Pinot Blanc.

- 2 tablespoons olive oil or salad oil
- 2 or 3 large pheasants (2½ to 3 lbs. *each*), cleaned, trimmed, cut into serving-sized pieces
- 1 cup *each* chopped onion and parsley
- 1 can (about 14 oz.) regular-strength chicken broth
- ½ cup **white wine**
- 3 sprigs fresh rosemary (or ½ teaspoon dried rosemary)
- 1 can (4 or 6 oz.) sliced mushrooms
- 6 tablespoons all-purpose flour
- Salt and pepper to taste

Heat oil in a Dutch oven over medium heat; brown pheasant pieces, a few at a time, on all sides. Discard excess fat. Return all pheasant to Dutch oven. Combine onion, parsley, chicken broth, wine, and rosemary; pour over pheasant. Cover pan and simmer until birds are fork tender, about 1 hour and 15 minutes for farm-raised pheasant; longer for wild birds.

To serve, remove pheasant to a warm platter and keep warm. Drain mushrooms, reserve liquid; add mushrooms to pan drippings. Mix together flour and reserved mushroom liquid until smooth; stir into pan drippings, quickly bring to a boil and cook until thickened. Season with salt and pepper to taste. Spoon sauce over pheasant or pass in a separate bowl. Makes 8 to 10 servings.

Venison Barbecue

Cold coffee, dry red wine, and mincemeat are the basis of the marinade for this venison roast. Use a wine such as Burgundy or a Zinfandel.

- 1 cup *each* cold coffee and **dry red wine**
- ½ cup lemon juice
- 1 teaspoon *each* ground ginger and salt
- 2 packages (9 oz. *each*) instant condensed mincemeat
- 2½ to 3-pound venison roast

In a large pan, combine coffee, wine, lemon juice, ginger, and salt. Break in the mincemeat and stir to mix well. Add venison and immerse. Cover and refrigerate overnight; turn meat occasionally.

Grease barbecue grill with small amount of shortening; place roast on grill about 4 to 6 inches over a drip pan surrounded by glowing coals; cover barbecue with hood or drape roast with heavy foil. Every 5 minutes or so baste meat with marinade. Allow about 25 minutes on each side for rare. Spoon any remaining marinade over meat before serving. Makes about 6 servings.

Capretto Sauté with Green Olives

Baby goat or kid is a flavorful meat popular and traditional with many Mexican, Spanish, Greek, and French families. In Italian it is called Capretto, and this is a recipe for the chops. Capretto is most apt to be available in the spring if ordered at Italian or Spanish meat markets or from goat dairy farms. Use a wine such as dry Sauterne or dry Semillon.

- 1½ to 2 pounds capretto chops
- 1 tablespoon olive oil
- ⅓ cup tomato sauce
- ¾ cup **dry white wine**
- 1 cup ripe green olives, drained

Brown the capretto chops on both sides in the olive oil in a large frying pan. Spread chops with tomato sauce and add the wine and green olives. Cover and simmer until olives are heated through, about 15 minutes. Serve immediately, topping with the pan juice and olives. Makes 4 to 6 servings of 2 to 3 chops each.

Rabbit in Red Wine

Tender young frying rabbits are available fresh or frozen. Their delicate texture lends itself very well to this flavorful sauce. Use a wine such as a Burgundy or a Gamay.

- 2 large onions
- 2 fryer rabbits (about 2½ lbs. *each*), cut up
- 1 bay leaf
- 2½ cups **dry red wine**
- 1 tablespoon red wine vinegar
- Juice of 1 lemon (about 3 tablespoons)
- ¾ teaspoon whole thyme
- ½ teaspoon salt
- ¼ teaspoon pepper
- 5 tablespoons butter or margarine
- 1 large tart apple, peeled and chopped
- 2 shallots, or large green onions, finely chopped
- 1 cup regular-strength beef broth
- 2 teaspoons cornstarch blended with 1 tablespoon water
- 1 teaspoon bottled brown gravy sauce

Peel one of the onions, slice it thinly, and separate into rings. Place rabbit, onion rings, and bay leaf in a large shallow bowl. Pour in a mixture of the wine, vinegar, lemon juice, thyme, salt, and pepper. Cover, and refrigerate for 24 to 36 hours.

Drain rabbit, reserving marinade and onion rings; discard bay leaf. Chop livers and sauté until lightly browned in 2 tablespoons of the butter in a saucepan. Chop remaining onion; add it with apple to livers. Sauté until onion is soft. Add 1 cup of the reserved marinade; simmer covered for 1 hour.

Meanwhile, melt remaining 3 tablespoons butter in a large frying pan. Brown rabbit pieces well on all sides. Add shallots, reserved onion rings, remaining marinade, and beef broth. Simmer, covered, for about 1 hour, until rabbit is tender. Remove rabbit from pan.

Purée liver mixture in blender. Stir liver purée, cornstarch mixture, and brown gravy sauce into liquid in pan. Cook, stirring constantly, until thickened. Add rabbit to sauce; simmer, covered, for about 10 minutes longer. Makes 6 to 8 servings.

Baked Buffalo

Buffalo cuts, occasionally available in supermarkets, are similar to beef, and can be cooked in much the same way. The taste, too, is often indistinguishable from beef, although buffalo tends to have a fuller, richer flavor and a darker red color. Use a wine such as a Zinfandel or a Cabernet Sauvignon.

3 pounds buffalo stew meat, cut in 1-inch cubes
2 cups finely chopped onion
2 cloves garlic, finely chopped
2 bay leaves
1½ teaspoons salt
¼ teaspoon pepper
⅓ cup salad oil
½ cup all-purpose flour
1½ cups *each* **dry red wine** and water
1 can (6 oz.) tomato paste
Hot cooked noodles or rice

Place buffalo, onion, garlic, and bay leaves in shallow baking pan; sprinkle with salt and pepper. Bake uncovered in a 425° oven for 10 minutes; reduce heat to 300° and continue baking about 30 minutes longer or until juices are released from meat.

Meanwhile, heat oil in a deep, covered, 3-quart pan that can go into the oven; stir in flour to form a smooth paste. Cook, stirring, until browned. Remove from heat; gradually stir in wine, water, and tomato paste until smooth. Add meat with its juices to the sauce, cover and bake in a 350° oven about 2 hours, or until meat is very tender. Serve over hot noodles or rice. Makes 6 servings.

Pieuvre à la Provençale

Octopus, one of the more exotic members of the shellfish family, is available in large seafood markets, Oriental or Italian markets. It may be fresh, but more likely it will be frozen. If the octopus is cooked, all you need to do is remove and discard the skin, then dice the meat and proceed as directed below; however, if the octopus requires cooking consult the instructions that follow the recipe. Use a wine such as a Chablis or a Pinot Blanc.

2 tablespoons salad oil
4 thinly sliced green onions (including tops)
1 clove whole garlic
⅛ teaspoon rosemary
¼ teaspoon thyme
1 tablespoon minced parsley
2 medium-sized tomatoes, peeled and diced
2 cups cooked and diced octopus
¾ cup **dry white wine**
Salt

Sauté in oil the onions, garlic, rosemary, thyme, parsley, and tomatoes until vegetables are soft. Add the octopus and wine. Pour all into a shallow 1½-quart casserole; bake in a 325° oven for 2 hours, stirring occasionally. Salt to taste. Makes 4 servings.

How to Cook Fresh or Fresh Frozen Octopus. Select a 1 to 5 pound octopus; thaw if frozen. If the octopus is whole, slit open the head cavity and discard the interior. Cut away and discard the beak (between legs); wash thoroughly. Separate legs and head and drop into a large quantity of boiling salted water. Cover and simmer gently until skin can be peeled or stripped from the flesh; usually takes about 30 minutes. Let octopus cool in cooking water. Remove and discard skin. Use meat as directed above.

Smoked Beef Tongue with Spiced Fruit Sauce

Tongue is available fresh, corned, and smoked. Choose one that is smoked to serve with this spicy sauce. Use a wine such as Burgundy, Gamay, or Gamay Beaujolais.

1 smoked beef tongue (about 3½ lbs.)
Water
1 medium-sized onion
2 carrots
1 stalk celery
1 bay leaf
½ teaspoon *each* whole black peppers, whole cloves, and whole allspice
1 cup canned, condensed beef consommé
1 cup water
½ cup **dry red wine**
Grated peel and juice of 1 orange and 1 lemon
1 can (13½ oz.) pineapple chunks, drained
½ cup *each* pitted dates and golden raisins
2 to 4 tablespoons firmly packed brown sugar
2 teaspoons prepared horseradish
1 tablespoon Worcestershire
½ teaspoon *each* ground ginger and ground cinnamon
2 tablespoons *each* melted butter and all-purpose flour

In a kettle, cover tongue with water; add onion, carrots, celery, bay leaf, whole black peppers, cloves, and allspice. Bring to a boil, cover and simmer very slowly about 3½ hours (1 hour per lb.) or until tongue is tender when pierced. Meanwhile combine consommé, the 1 cup water, wine, peel and juice of orange and lemon, pineapple, dates, raisins, sugar, horseradish, Worcestershire, ginger, and cinnamon. Simmer for 15 minutes. Blend butter and flour, mix with some of the sauce and stir into remaining sauce. Bring to a boil and cook, stirring, until slightly thickened. Peel skin from warm tongue. Slice tongue thinly across grain and place in a baking pan. Pour sauce over tongue and bake in a 350° oven for 25 minutes. Makes 8 servings.

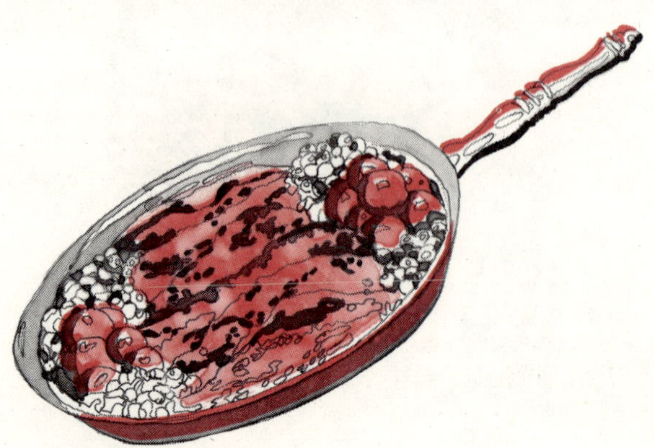

Braised Sweetbreads with Vegetables

Sweetbreads develop a rich subtle flavor when braised with a *mirepoix* (chopped vegetable mixture). This entrée will hold well in a warm oven another hour after cooking should dinner be delayed. Use a wine such as dry Sauterne or Chablis.

2 pounds sweetbreads, prepared (directions follow)
Water, salt, and lemon juice
1 large onion
3 medium-sized carrots
3 stalks celery
1 cup finely diced ham
3 to 4 tablespoons butter or margarine
1 bay leaf
2 tablespoons chopped fresh parsley
½ teaspoon thyme
1 cup regular-strength chicken broth
⅔ cup **dry white wine**

Wash sweetbreads well in cool water, rinsing until water is clear. Cover with water adding 1 teaspoon salt and 1 tablespoon lemon juice for each quart of water. Bring to a boil and simmer about 15 minutes. Drain and plunge sweetbreads immediately into cold water to stop cooking; drain again. With your fingers and the point of a sharp knife, remove as much of the white connecting membrane as possible and break sweetbreads into bite-sized pieces. If not used immediately, place in cold water and refrigerate. Use within 36 hours.

Finely chop onion, carrots, and celery. Sauté the vegetables and ham in the butter in a heatproof casserole or small Dutch oven until vegetables are soft. Add bay leaf, parsley, and thyme. Remove pan from heat and arrange sweetbreads over the vegetable mixture. Pour the broth and wine over all. Return to heat and bring the liquid to a boil; simmer about 4 minutes to reduce the liquid. Cover and bake in a 350° oven about 40 minutes. If you want the sweetbreads browned on top, remove the cover; if you prefer them light in color, leave covered, bake 20 minutes more. Makes 4 to 6 servings.

Frogs' Legs Mornay

Frozen frogs' legs, most available in fish markets, are skinned and ready to use; just thaw, rinse, and if you like, separate legs. Here they are served with a quick Mornay cheese sauce flavored with a wine such as a Chablis or a Chardonnay.

All-purpose flour
4 pairs medium-sized frogs' legs, thawed if frozen, and separated into individual legs, if desired
About 4 tablespoons butter
1 garlic clove, split
1 or 2 large mushrooms, sliced
2 tablespoons **dry white wine**
1 cup canned white sauce
⅓ cup shredded Gruyère cheese
¼ cup whipping cream
Shredded Parmesan cheese to taste

Flour the frogs' legs lightly and cook in butter over medium-high heat, along with the garlic, until they are a delicate brown. Place 2 pairs of frogs' legs in each of 2 buttered individual casseroles. Sauté mushrooms in remaining butter (add more if needed) until limp. Arrange over frogs' legs in each casserole. In a saucepan blend wine, white sauce, and Gruyère cheese. Cook over medium heat, stirring, until hot and cheese is melted. Whip cream until stiff and fold into hot sauce. Pour Mornay sauce equally over frogs' legs. Sprinkle with shredded Parmesan cheese. Brown under the broiler. Serve hot. Makes 2 servings.

Chile Beans and Heart Azteca

Use a wine such as Mountain Red or Zinfandel.

About ½ cup **dry red wine** (or more if desired)
1 teaspoon *each* salt and whole oregano
½ teaspoon chile powder
1 beef heart, trimmed of fat and sliced in finger-sized pieces
2 slices bacon
1 medium-sized onion, chopped
1 can (about 1 lb.) chile beans

Combine the wine with the salt, oregano, and chile powder. Pour over the heart slices in a bowl and marinate about 30 minutes. Fry bacon in a large frying pan until crisp; remove bacon and set aside, leaving drippings in the pan; sauté onion in drippings until soft; push to one side. Drain heart, save marinade.

Lightly brown heart on all sides in the bacon drippings. Pour over the reserved marinade. Place bacon slices on meat, cover, and simmer gently until heart is tender, 2½ to 3 hours; add more wine if needed. Stir in the canned beans and cook about 15 minutes longer. Makes 4 to 6 servings.

German-Style Kidneys

The secret to kidney preparation is cooking them until just firm (when interior pink color has disappeared). They toughen when overcooked. Vermouth or Sherry flavors the sauce.

2 pounds beef kidneys (about 2)
1 bay leaf
Salt and water
3 tablespoons butter
1 medium-sized onion, thinly sliced
½ pound mushrooms, sliced
1½ teaspoons sugar
2 tablespoons *each* vinegar and all-purpose flour
⅓ cup **dry Vermouth** or **dry Sherry**
1 cup regular-strength beef broth
1 tablespoon tomato catsup
¼ teaspoon whole thyme
Hot cooked noodles

Cut away fatty membrane from kidneys; cut kidneys in ¼-inch-thick slices. Place in a small pan with bay leaf and add enough salted water to cover generously. Bring to boiling and simmer gently for 5 minutes. Drain, discard bay, rinse kidneys with cool water, and set aside.

In a wide frying pan, melt 1 tablespoon of the butter, add the onion and mushrooms and cook, stirring, over moderately-high heat until vegetables are lightly browned. Remove from pan and set aside.

Sprinkle sugar in the frying pan and place over high heat until it melts and turns deep amber in color. Immediately pour in vinegar and add remaining 2 tablespoons butter; boil, stirring, until most liquid has evaporated.

Add kidneys to pan, blend in the flour, add Vermouth, broth, vegetables, catsup, and thyme and quickly bring to boiling, stirring; cook until sauce is thickened slightly. Salt if needed. Serve spooned over noodles. Makes 4 to 6 servings.

WAYS WITH CHEESE AND EGGS

Fondue to Omelets

Possibly the best known and certainly one of the most popular cheese dishes for entertaining is fondue. The one in this chapter is quite authentically Swiss. Cheese and wine, as favorite combinations for eating, are equally compatible when cooked together. Eggs, also, combine easily with wine in soufflés, omelets, and in sauces to serve with eggs. It is wise to leave the red wines on the shelf, for they can give eggs an unappetizing blue-gray cast.

Basque Oven Omelet

These individual oven omelets can be served as a lunch or breakfast main dish because they are made hearty by cheese and Canadian bacon.

- 8 eggs
- ⅓ cup sour cream
- 2 tablespoons **dry Vermouth** or **dry Sherry**
- ¼ teaspoon salt
- 2 cups coarsely shredded Swiss cheese
- ½ cup sliced pimiento-stuffed olives
- 8 thin slices cooked Canadian bacon (about ½ lb.)
- 2 teaspoons butter or margarine, melted

In a mixing bowl beat eggs until foamy; mix in sour cream, Vermouth, and salt. Mix in the cheese and olives. Spoon into 4 buttered 5-inch round baking dishes. Arrange 2 slices bacon on top of each omelet. Drizzle butter over the tops of the omelets.

Bake in a 350° oven for 25 minutes, or until set and puffy. Makes 4 servings.

Mushroom Soufflé

This soufflé is substantial enough to be an entrée for a light supper.

- 5 tablespoons butter or margarine
- 1 pound mushrooms, chopped
- 3 shallots or green onions (white part only), finely chopped
- 5 tablespoons all-purpose flour
- ⅓ cup **Cream Sherry** or **Madeira**
- ¾ cup milk
- 1 teaspoon salt
- 9 eggs, separated

Melt butter in a large saucepan. Add mushrooms and shallots and simmer rapidly, stirring, until all liquid has cooked away. Stir in flour; blend in gradually the Sherry, milk, and salt. Cook, stirring, until thickened. Remove from heat and beat in the egg yolks. Whip egg whites until they hold short distinct peaks. Fold about half of the whites very thoroughly into the sauce. Fold in remaining whites as thoroughly as you like.

Pour into a well-buttered 2½-quart soufflé dish. Run tip of spoon or knife around top within an inch or two of the rim if you want the soufflé to form a top-knot. Bake in a 375° oven for 40 minutes. Makes 6 servings.

Swiss Custard Ramekins

This make-ahead brunch dish resembles the old fashioned oven cheese fondue. White wine and cheese custard saturates the buttered bread base and puffs up when baked. Use a wine such as dry Sauterne or a Chablis.

- 4 slices white bread
- Soft butter
- 3 eggs
- 1½ cups half-and-half or milk
- ½ cup **dry white wine**
- ⅛ teaspoon *each* salt and dry mustard
- 2 cups shredded Swiss cheese
- 2 green onions, including part of tops, finely chopped (optional)

Spread bread with softened butter and arrange in four small baking dishes or ramekins. Beat eggs until foamy and mix in half-and-half, wine, salt, and mustard. Distribute cheese over the bread and pour over the custard. Sprinkle chopped onions on top, if desired. Cover and chill at least 30 minutes or as long as overnight.

Bake in a 350° oven for 20 to 30 minutes, or until custard is set and bread puffs up. Serve immediately. Makes 4 servings.

Cheese Fondue

Kirsch is the classic punch added to cheese fondue, but it can be omitted if desired. Use a wine such as Chablis or Traminer.

- 1 clove garlic, cut in half
- 2 cups **light dry white wine**
- ½ pound imported Swiss cheese (Emmental), shredded
- ½ pound Swiss Gruyère or Danish Samsoe, shredded
- 1 tablespoon cornstarch
- 1 teaspoon dry mustard (optional)
- 3 tablespoons Kirsch
- Freshly ground nutmeg and pepper, to taste
- 1 small loaf French bread, cut in 1-inch cubes with some crust on each

Rub the sides and bottom of the fondue pot with the cut garlic. Add wine, and heat slowly until bubbles form and slowly rise to the surface. Combine the two cheeses, cornstarch, and mustard. Add cheese mixture, a spoonful at a time; stir slowly and continuously until all the cheese is blended into a smooth sauce—it should bubble very slowly.

Stir in Kirsch a tablespoon at a time, and again bring to a slow boil. Fondue may separate if the heat gets too high at any time. Sprinkle with nutmeg and pepper, to taste. Take to the table with bread cubes, and adjust heat so fondue keeps bubbling slowly. Fondue can be thinned down with a little heated wine if it gets too thick. Makes about 4 servings.

Macaroni and Cheese

This is a speedy variation of an old standby recipe. Simply melt and thin the cheese in a frying pan while boiling the macaroni; add macaroni to the cheese sauce, then slip it under the broiler to brown the top. Use a wine such as dry Sauterne or Sauvignon Blanc.

- 8 ounces macaroni or noodles
- Boiling, salted water
- Olive oil or salad oil
- 12 ounces cheese (Cheddar, Gruyère, Samsoe, or teleme)
- ½ cup **dry white wine**
- Salt
- About 1 cup seasoned croutons (optional)

Cook macaroni in boiling, salted water to cover, following directions on the package. Don't overcook it. When tender, pour into a colander to drain until cheese is ready.

Meanwhile coat the bottom of a medium-sized frying pan with oil and place over low heat. Put in cheese, stir, and when it starts to melt, add liquid, a little at a time, just enough to make a creamy, smooth sauce.

Remove from heat as soon as cheese has melted and blend in the hot macaroni and salt to taste. Sprinkle with croutons, if desired. Place pan about 2 inches below broiler and broil 1 to 2 minutes, until lightly browned. Serve at once. Makes about 4 servings.

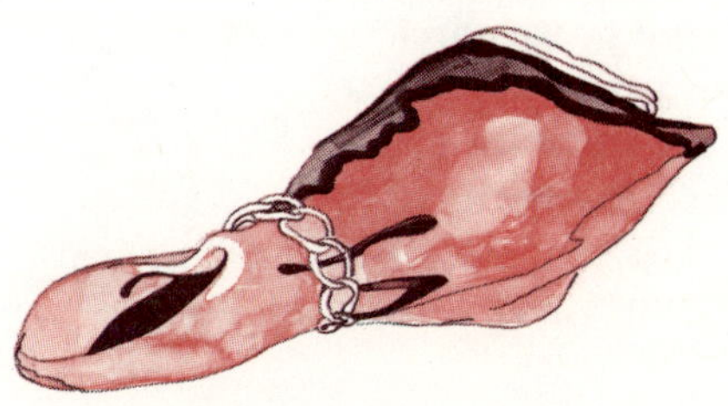

VEGETABLE SURPRISES

Asparagus to Zucchini

Many a vegetable dish takes to wine. Carrots in wine sauce; Sherry with yams or onions; Port with cabbage; tomatoes with Vermouth. The vegetables, thusly defined, have refreshingly different character.

You might elect to serve one of the chilled-wine vegetable dishes in the role of first-course or salad as well as a meat accompaniment.

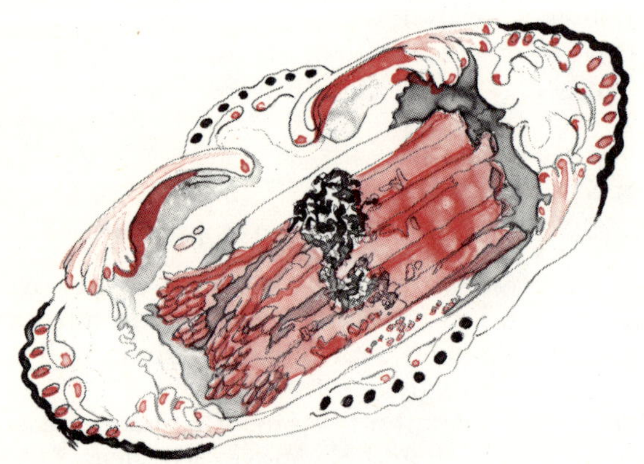

Beets with Mandarin Oranges

Consider this dish when your menu needs a brightly colored vegetable. Use a wine such as Mountain White or Chablis.

- ⅓ cup sugar
- 1½ teaspoons cornstarch
- 2 tablespoons lemon juice
- ⅓ cup **dry white wine**
- 2 tablespoons butter
- 1 can (11 oz.) mandarin oranges, drained
- 2 cans (1 lb. *each*) small whole beets, drained

In a saucepan combine sugar and cornstarch. Add lemon juice and wine; stir until well blended. Add butter and cook over medium heat, stirring, until it boils and thickens, and becomes clear. Remove from heat. (At this point you can lightly combine drained oranges and beets in a greased 1½-quart casserole. Pour over the thickened sauce. Cover casserole and refrigerate.) Add oranges and beets; cover and cook slowly just until heated through. (If refrigerated, bake, covered, in a 350° oven about 15 minutes or until hot through.) Makes 6 to 8 servings.

Red Cabbage in Port

- 1 small head (about 1 lb.) red cabbage, finely shredded
- About 1 cup **Tinta** or **Ruby Port wine**
- 1½ teaspoons vinegar
- 1 medium-sized apple, peeled, cored, and thinly sliced
- Salt

Combine cabbage, all of the wine, and vinegar in a large pan. Add the apple and bring to a boil. Cover pan and simmer gently for 1½ hours, stirring occasionally; add a little more Port if cabbage cooks dry. Salt to taste and turn into a serving dish. Makes 2 to 3 servings.

Creamy Celery

- 3 tablespoons butter or margarine
- 3 cups thinly sliced raw celery
- 3 tablespoons all-purpose flour
- 1½ to 2 cups milk
- 1 tablespoon **dry Sherry**
- Salt and pepper

Melt butter in a heavy frying pan; add celery, cover,

and cook over low heat, stirring occasionally, for about 5 minutes, or until celery is slightly tender. Add flour and stir until well blended; add milk gradually and cook, stirring constantly, until mixture is thickened and smooth; stir in Sherry and add salt and pepper to taste. Makes 6 servings.

Sherry-Cheese Onion Rings

- 6 large onions, sliced and separated into rings
- ½ teaspoon *each* sugar, salt, and freshly ground pepper
- 5 tablespoons butter
- ½ cup **dry** or **medium Sherry**
- 2 tablespoons grated Parmesan cheese

Season onion rings with salt, pepper, and sugar. In a wide frying pan, sauté onion rings in butter, tossing lightly to stir, until limp. Add the Sherry and cook rapidly for 2 to 3 minutes to reduce liquid. Sprinkle with Parmesan cheese and serve. Makes 6 servings.

Yam Soufflé

- 3 cups mashed cooked yams or sweet potatoes (unseasoned)
- ⅓ cup **medium** or **dry Sherry**
- 1¼ cups half-and-half
- 6 tablespoons melted butter or margarine
- 1½ teaspoons grated orange peel
- ⅛ teaspoon *each* pepper and nutmeg
- 1 teaspoon salt
- 2 tablespoons firmly packed brown sugar
- 6 eggs, separated

Combine in the mixer bowl the mashed yams, Sherry, half-and-half, butter, orange peel, pepper, nutmeg, salt, and sugar; beat with an electric mixer until blended and smooth. Add egg yolks and beat in thoroughly. This much can be done ahead and the mixture held at room temperature for several hours. Just before baking whip egg whites until they hold short, distinct, moist peaks; carefully fold into potato mixture.

Spoon equally into 12 well buttered, individual soufflé dishes (5 to 6 oz. size) and bake in a 375° oven about 20 minutes. (Or use 2½ qt. soufflé dish and bake 45 minutes.) Serve immediately. Makes 12 servings.

String Beans with Herbs

Use any dry white wine you might have on hand.

- 1 pound green beans, strings and ends removed, then cut in thin slivers
- Boiling salted water
- 2 tablespoons salad oil
- 1 small onion, thinly sliced
- 1 clove garlic, cut in half
- 1 large tomato, peeled
- 1 tablespoon **dry white wine**
- 1 tablespoon *each* minced green pepper fresh parsley, and celery
- ½ teaspoon crumbled marjoram
- Pinch of rosemary
- Salt and pepper

Cook beans in a small amount of boiling salted water for about 15 minutes, uncovered, or until tender; drain. Heat oil and gently cook onion and garlic for about 10 minutes. Slice tomato into pan and add wine, green pepper, parsley, celery, marjoram, and rosemary; simmer for 10 minutes; add to beans. Cover pan and simmer 5 minutes longer. Remove garlic. Season to taste with salt and pepper and serve. Makes 4 servings.

Tomatoes Provençal

Use dry Vermouth or a wine such as Chablis.

- 4 tablespoons butter
- 2 tablespoons *each* finely chopped shallots (or green onions, including part of tops), and parsley
- ½ teaspoon sugar
- 3 tablespoons **dry Vermouth** or **dry white wine**
- 3 medium-sized tomatoes, peeled, cored, quartered, and seeded
- 2 small cloves garlic, minced or mashed
- Salt and pepper

Melt 2 of the tablespoons butter in a pan and add the shallots, parsley, sugar, and Vermouth. Bring mixture to boiling, stirring occasionally.

Add tomatoes to pan, mixing gently just until heated through. Add the remaining tablespoons butter and the garlic, stirring until butter melts. Remove at once from heat, season with salt and pepper to taste, and serve at once. Makes 4 to 6 servings.

Spicy Zucchini

Use a wine such as a Chablis or dry Sauterne.

- 1 medium-sized onion, finely chopped
- 1 clove garlic, minced or mashed
- ⅓ cup chopped parsley
- 2 tablespoons salad oil
- 1 pound zucchini
- 1 can (8 oz. size) tomato sauce
- ¼ cup **dry white wine**
- 1 tablespoon sugar
- ½ teaspoon *each* nutmeg and salt
- ¼ teaspoon *each* cinnamon and pepper
- ½ cup grated Parmesan cheese

Sauté onion, garlic, and parsley in the oil in a large frying pan until onions are limp. Slice zucchini into ⅛ to ¼-inch rounds; add to pan and simmer on low heat, covered, for 5 minutes. Stir in tomato sauce, wine, sugar, nutmeg, salt, cinnamon, and pepper. Cover and simmer until zucchini is tender (about 5 minutes), stirring frequently. Stir in the cheese just before serving. Makes 4 servings.

Summer Squash with Mushrooms

Either Madeira, White Port, or Cream Sherry can be used in this squash and mushroom combination. The dish holds well if dinner is delayed.

- 2 pounds small pattypan or zucchini squash
- 1 pound medium-sized mushrooms
- Salt
- Water
- 3 to 4 tablespoons butter
- ¼ cup **Madeira, White Port**, or **Cream Sherry**
- Pepper

Thorougly wash squash, trim off ends and cut into ½-inch chunks. Wash mushrooms and slice off bottom end of the stem. Cut mushrooms into the same size chunks as the squash. Put squash into a pan, barely cover with salted water, cover pan and bring to a boil, then uncover and cook 10 to 15 minutes, or until barely tender. Meanwhile put mushrooms in a shallow pan with butter and wine. Simmer 10 minutes, covered.

Drain squash thoroughly, add mushrooms and juice; salt and pepper to taste. Serve at once or cover, keep warm, up to an hour, before serving. Makes 8 servings.

Lima Beans with Curry Sauce

This vegetable dish can be kept warm in the oven up to an hour, or reheated before serving. Use Sherry or a wine such as Chablis.

- 1 large package (1 lb. 4 oz.) frozen lima beans
- Boiling salted water
- 2 slices bacon, diced
- 1 medium-sized onion, minced
- 1 small clove garlic, mashed
- 1 teaspoon curry powder
- 1 can (10½ oz.) condensed cream of mushroom soup
- 2 tablespoons **dry Sherry** or **dry white wine**
- ½ cup sour cream
- 1 can (3½ oz.) French-fried onions

Cook lima beans in a small amount of boiling water until just tender, about 15 minutes; drain well. In a frying pan, fry bacon pieces until crisp; remove bacon with a slotted spoon, and reserve. In the drippings, sauté onion, garlic, and curry until onion is soft, about 5 minutes. Stir in soup, Sherry, and sour cream; heat to just under boiling point. Stir in beans and reserved bacon; heat through again. Turn into a serving bowl, cover and keep warm. Heat onions in a frying pan, stirring over moderate heat, then sprinkle over beans to serve. Makes 6 to 8 servings.

Carrots in Wine Sauce

- 8 medium-sized carrots, peeled
- 3 tablespoons butter or margarine
- 6 to 8 green onions, including part of tops, thinly sliced
- 1/4 teaspoon salt
- 1 tablespoon water
- 4 teaspoons all-purpose flour
- 2/3 cup half-and-half or milk
- 3 tablespoons **Sherry** or **Madeira**
- Finely chopped fresh parsley

Slice carrots about 1/8 inch thick. In a frying pan with a cover, melt the butter. Add the carrots and onions and sauté on medium-high heat about 3 minutes. Add the salt and water; cover and cook gently until carrots are almost tender, about 7 minutes. Sprinkle with flour, and cook, stirring, until flour is bubbly. Remove from heat and gradually stir in cream and wine; cook, stirring, until thickened. Serve immediately. Spoon into a serving dish and sprinkle with parsley. Makes 4 to 6 servings.

Asparagus in Wine

Use a wine such as a Rhine, Riesling, or Sylvaner.

- 2 pounds asparagus
- Boiling salted water
- 1/4 cup *each* butter or margarine and **dry white wine**
- 1/2 teaspoon salt
- 1/4 teaspoon pepper
- 1/3 cup grated Parmesan cheese

Wash asparagus; snap off and discard tough ends. Lay spears in a large shallow pan; pour over them enough boiling salted water to cover. Cook over high heat until water resumes boiling; reduce heat, and simmer until tender-crisp, about 4 to 8 minutes. Drain well and arrange spears in a buttered, shallow 1-quart casserole. Melt butter; stir in wine and pour over asparagus. Sprinkle with salt, pepper, and cheese. Bake in a 425° oven for 15 minutes. Makes 4 to 6 servings.

Sherried Peas and Mushrooms

- 2 cans (3 or 4 oz. size) sliced mushrooms
- 2 tablespoons butter
- 1/4 teaspoon crumbled marjoram
- 1/8 teaspoon nutmeg
- 2 tablespoons **Sherry**
- 2 packages (10 oz. *each*) frozen petit peas

Drain liquid from mushrooms and reserve. In a wide pan heat mushrooms in melted butter until sizzling, then stir in the marjoram, nutmeg, and Sherry. Break apart frozen peas and pour into pan with mushrooms, turn off heat and let stand at least 20 minutes to thaw. Just before serving add 2 tablespoons of the reserved mushroom liquid to peas and bring to boiling, stirring occasionally. Makes 6 generous servings.

Cold Vegetable Compote

Sherry is the accent for this chilled turnip, carrot, and cucumber trio.

- 1 cup *each* finely chopped turnips and carrots
- 2 medium-sized cucumbers, peeled and diced
- 1 teaspoon salt
- 3 tablespoons *each* sugar and vinegar
- 4 teaspoons **dry** or **medium Sherry**

Combine turnips, carrots, and cucumbers. Sprinkle with salt and let stand 2 hours. Stir in sugar, vinegar, and Sherry; chill overnight. Makes about 1 quart or 4 to 6 servings.

A VINTAGE FINISH

Fruit Desserts, Pastries, Puddings

A dessert flamed at the table makes a dramatic conclusion to any dinner. The technique is clearly explained with the recipes—such as in the classic variation of a jubilee with fresh strawberries. Wine is used to flavor desserts, puddings, cakes, and to mellow and enrich fruit cakes.

Strawberries Jubilee

In this dessert, whole strawberries and orange slices are served over ice cream balls and then flamed at the table.

- 1 quart vanilla ice cream
- 1 large navel orange, peeled, and thinly sliced
- 1 can (6 oz.) thawed frozen orange juice concentrate (undiluted)
- 1½ cups whole strawberries, washed and hulled
- 3 tablespoons **brandy**

Scoop ice cream into balls and refreeze, covered. (Or pack ice cream into a fancy mold and refreeze.) Cut each slice of orange in half. Just before serving, warm the orange juice concentrate, orange slices, and strawberries in a chafing dish. Warm the brandy, ignite, and spoon flaming over the warmed fruit sauce. Spoon sauce over the ice cream balls, placed in dessert bowls, or onto serving size portions of ice cream cut from the ice cream mold, which you have unmolded on a platter. Makes 6 servings.

Eggnog Ice Cream with Flaming Mincemeat Sauce

Eggnog, a flavor synonymous with the good cheer and merriment at Christmastime makes a delicious all-year treat when captured in homemade refrigerator frozen ice cream. The flaming sauce is an optional element that you might prefer to reserve for party occasions.

- 2 cups milk
- 1 teaspoon ground or grated nutmeg
- 6 egg yolks
- ¾ cup sugar
- ½ teaspoon salt
- ½ cup **medium Sherry**
- 2 cups (1 pt.) whipping cream
- Flaming mincemeat sauce (recipe follows)

Heat milk with the nutmeg in the top of a double boiler. Beat the egg yolks with ½ cup of the sugar and salt. Add some of the hot milk to yolks then stir all back into the top of the double boiler and place over hot water. Cook, stirring over slightly simmering water (just a few bubbles around pan sides), until mixture coats a metal spoon in a smooth even layer. Remove at once from heat and set double boiler top in cold water to cool. Stir in Sherry. Turn into freezer trays; freeze until consistency of soft ice cream. Turn out into a chilled bowl and beat until smooth and fluffy. Beat cream with the remaining ¼ cup sugar until stiff; fold into the frozen mixture. Freeze until firm. Serve scoops of the ice cream with flaming mincemeat sauce if desired. Makes 1½ quarts.

Flaming Mincemeat Sauce:

Mix together 2 cups (1 pt.) mincemeat with 1 cup cranberry juice cocktail. Heat until simmering in a chafing dish. Warm ½ cup brandy in a small container and, at the table, ignite brandy and pour into hot mincemeat; spoon sauce until flames die, then spoon over eggnog ice cream. Makes 3 cups.

Cantaloupe à la Mode with Port-Blueberry Sauce

- ½ cup sugar
- 1 tablespoon cornstarch
- 3 thin lemon slices
- ¾ cup **Tinta** or **Ruby Port**
- 1½ to 2 cups blueberries (fresh or unsugared frozen)
- Firm vanilla ice cream
- Cantaloupe rings or halves

In a small saucepan, combine sugar, cornstarch, lemon slices, and wine. Bring to a boil and cook, stirring, until thickened and clear, about 5 minutes. Remove lemon, add blueberries, and chill thoroughly. Spoon ice cream into melon rings or halves, and top with the chilled blueberry sauce. Makes about 1¾ cups sauce, enough for 6 to 8 servings.

Fruit Wine Ice

Fruit and berry wines make refreshing ices as freezing seems to intensify their natural fruit flavors. It is especially true of these fruit wines: apple, apricot, cherry, pear, plum, blackberry, currant, loganberry, raspberry, and strawberry.

The ices are delicious served separately or in combination as desserts—but when the fresh fruit is in season try pairing it with its own flavor ice. Also consider pairing fruit wine ices with fresh fruits in flavor combinations you enjoy in all fresh fruits.

It is important that the wine contain about 12 per cent alcohol with no added sweetener; extra sugar or more alcohol interferes with freezing.

- 1¾ cups **fruit** or **berry wine**
- ¾ cup water
- ½ cup sugar
- Food coloring (optional)

In a bowl stir wine, water, and sugar until sugar is completely dissolved. Pour into a shallow metal pan, cover, and freeze at 0° or colder until solid. Remove ice from freezer and break up into small pieces with a wooden spoon (if too hard, let stand 5 to 10 minutes); turn into the large bowl of an electric mixer. Beat at lowest speed until slushy, then gradually increase speed until mixture becomes smooth but not melted.

Beat in a few drops of food coloring if you wish to intensify the color (about ¼ teaspoon red food coloring turns blackberry or cherry wine ice rosy). Spoon back into freezing tray, cover tightly, and freeze. Makes 6 to 8 servings.

Pineapple with Port Sauce

The pineapple shell is the natural container for this.

- ¼ cup sugar
- 1 tablespoon cornstarch
- 1 cup **Ruby Port**
- 1 tablespoon *each* lemon juice and frozen orange juice concentrate, undiluted
- 1 large pineapple
- 1 quart pineapple sherbet
- Mint sprigs

In a small pan mix together the sugar and cornstarch. Blend in Port, lemon juice, and orange juice concentrate. Stirring constantly, bring to a boil and cook until clear and thickened. Chill.

Cut pineapple lengthwise, into two unequal halves so that the crown with leaves is all on the larger shell. Use a grapefruit knife, cut out the fruit preserving the pineapple shells intact; remove core, and cut the fruit into large pieces. Place fruit and juice in a bowl; chill. Chill the larger shell with the leaves on it and discard the leafless portion. Scoop sherbet into balls and refreeze, covered, until serving time.

When ready to serve, measure out ½ cup of the pineapple juice and stir into the Port sauce; pour into a serving pitcher. Spoon pineapple cubes and sherbet balls into the chilled pineapple shell. Garnish with mint. Serve from the shell into dessert bowls. Pass the sauce. Makes 6 servings.

Festa Zabaglione

A combination of Sherry and white wine replaces the more typical Marsala in this whipped egg foam dessert from Italy. If you use a Zabaglione pan you can cook this showpiece dessert at the table. Use a wine such as dry Sauterne or a dry Semillon.

6 egg yolks
5 tablespoons sugar
¼ cup **dry Sherry**
¼ cup **white wine**

Combine yolks with sugar in the top of a double boiler. Add Sherry and wine, and beat together using a wire whip. Place double boiler over water that is barely bubbling, or Zabaglione pan over an alcohol flame and whip constantly until mixture leaves a trail behind the whip, about 5 minutes. Serve immediately. Makes 4 servings.

Bombe Italienne

Marsala or Tawny Port, anise, and candied fruit play important roles in developing the flavors of this elegant dessert.

½ cup dried currants
½ cup **Marsala** or **Tawny Port**
½ cup pine nuts or chopped or slivered almonds
4 eggs
⅛ teaspoon salt
1 cup sugar
½ cup water
¼ cup finely chopped candied lemon or orange peel
1½ teaspoons crushed anise seed or a few drops anise flavoring
2 cups whipping cream
Garnish of whipped cream, candied fruits and nuts

Combine currants and wine in a pan and heat slowly to simmering; remove from heat and let currants stand in the wine until cool and plump. Put pine nuts in a shallow pan and place in a 350° oven, stirring occasionally until lightly browned; cool.

Using the large bowl of your mixer, beat the eggs with salt until foamy. Combine sugar and water in the top of a 2-quart double boiler. Heat to boiling over direct heat and boil for 3 minutes without stirring. Immediately pour this mixture in a fine stream into the beaten eggs, beating constantly at a high speed.

Pour this mixture back into the top of the double boiler and cook over simmering water, stirring constantly with a wooden spoon, until the mixture is slightly thickened. Remove from heat, set the pan in a bowl of cold water, and continue stirring until mixture is cooled. Stir in currants and wine, pine nuts, candied citrus peel, and anise seeds or flavoring. Whip cream until stiff and fold into egg mixture; pour into a bombe mold. Cover tightly with foil, and freeze immediately until firm. To unmold, dip mold very quickly into hot water; dry mold and invert on a chilled serving platter. Garnish with whipped cream, nuts, and candied fruit. Makes about 1¾ quarts, or 8 to 10 servings.

Rhubarb Sauce

Use a wine such as Burgundy or a Gamay; or a Rosé. Spoon over vanilla ice cream.

½ cup **dry red wine** or **Rosé**
1 package (12 oz.) frozen rhubarb or 1½ to 2 cups fresh rhubarb, cut up
¾ cup sugar
⅛ teaspoon salt
1 tablespoon cornstarch

Bring the wine just to a boil in a saucepan. Add rhubarb and simmer until thawed or just tender, about 5 minutes. Blend sugar, salt, and cornstarch; stir into rhubarb. Cook, stirring, until the sauce is thickened and clear. Cool. Makes about 1¾ cups or 4 servings.

Curried Bananas

A sweet curry sauce coats these dessert bananas as they bake. Use a wine such as Rhine wine or Riesling.

½ cup *each* orange juice and **dry white wine**
½ cup firmly packed light brown sugar
3 tablespoons melted butter
2 tablespoons lemon juice
¾ teaspoon curry powder
4 to 6 large, green-tipped bananas, peeled and cut in half lengthwise

Combine orange juice, wine, brown sugar, butter, lemon juice, and curry powder in a small pan and simmer until syrupy (about ⅓ original volume). Arrange halved bananas in a buttered 9 by 13-inch shallow baking dish leaving space between the halves. Pour on the reduced sauce and bake uncovered in a 350° oven for 20 minutes, basting frequently. Makes 4 to 6 servings.

Wine-Poached Babcock Peaches

The early small Babcock, a particularly flavorful though not perfectly beautiful peach, performs deliciously when poached. Use a wine such as a fruity Chenin Blanc or sweet Sauterne.

- ¼ cup mild honey
- 1 cup **slightly sweet white wine**
- 1 cup water
- 2 thin slices from a whole lemon
- 4 to 6 Babcock peaches, halved, pitted, and peeled

Combine in a saucepan the honey, wine, and water. Add lemon slices and peach halves. Bring to simmering, and simmer gently until peaches are tender, about 5 to 10 minutes. Chill in the poaching liquid and serve peaches with some of the liquid spooned over. Makes 4 servings.

Cinnamon Pears in Wine

Baked whole pears in a red wine sauce make a sophisticated finale for a dinner party. Use a wine such as Burgundy or Claret.

- 6 large Winter Nellis or Bosc pears
- 1 cup **dry red wine**
- ⅓ cup sugar
- 3 tablespoons thawed frozen undiluted orange juice concentrate
- ½ stick whole cinnamon (about a 2-inch piece)

Wash pears and leave whole, unpeeled. Place stem end up in a deep baking dish. Mix together the wine, sugar, and orange concentrate and pour over pears. Add cinnamon stick. Cover and bake in a 400° oven for 20 minutes. Remove cover and bake 30 minutes longer, or until tender; baste occasionally. Serve warm or chilled. Makes 6 servings.

Lemon Wine Chiffon

For a refreshing low-calorie dessert, try this airy Dutch pudding. It must be served within about 6 hours; on longer standing the foam begins to noticeably break down. Use a wine such as Riesling or Traminer.

- 4 eggs, separated
- 8 tablespoons sugar
- Juice and grated peel of 1 lemon
- ½ cup **dry white wine**
- ⅛ teaspoon *each* salt and cream of tartar

Beat egg yolks until thick and lemon colored in the top of a double boiler. Gradually beat in 6 tablespoons of the sugar, lemon juice and peel, and the wine. Place over hot water, and stirring constantly, cook until thickened. Remove from heat. Beat egg whites until foamy, add salt and cream of tartar, and beat until stiff; beat in the remaining 2 tablespoons sugar. Immediately fold the meringue into the hot lemon sauce. Spoon into dessert dishes or champagne glasses and chill. Serve in 6 hours or less. Garnish with a sprig of mint if you wish. Makes 6 servings.

Apples Rosé with Honey Whip

A spicy uncooked meringue tops these baked apples filled with Mandarin orange sections. Use a wine such as Rosé or Grenache Rosé.

- 6 large baking apples
- ½ cup *each* orange juice and **Rosé**
- ¾ cup sugar
- 2 sticks whole cinnamon, *each* 3 to 4 inches long
- 1 can (11 oz.) mandarin oranges
- Honey Whip (directions follow)

Core apples and pare off 1-inch of the peel around upper part of the apple. Arrange peeled sections up, side by side, in a baking dish. In a saucepan combine orange juice, wine, sugar, and cinnamon sticks (broken into pieces); simmer just until sugar dissolves, and pour over apples. Bake in a 350° oven for 30 to 40 minutes, or until apples are barely tender when pierced with a fork. Drain oranges, and spoon several orange sections inside the cavity of each apple. Baste with pan juices, and continue baking 5 minutes longer.

Honey Whip:

1 egg white
¼ cup honey
⅛ teaspoon nutmeg
½ cup whipping cream (optional)

Beat egg white until soft peaks form; then gradually add honey, beating until stiff. Beat in nutmeg. Serve at room temperature. For a creamy version, fold in whipped cream and chill before serving. Makes 6 servings.

Madeira Cake

Allow the currants to plump in the Madeira one hour before you start this cake.

About 1¼ cups **Madeira**
⅔ cup dried currants
½ cup *each* butter and shortening
2½ cups sugar
6 eggs
4 cups unsifted all-purpose flour
1 teaspoon soda
½ teaspoon salt
1 teaspoon *each* ground cinnamon, ground cloves, and ground nutmeg
½ cup milk
1½ tablespoons lemon juice
Powdered sugar

In a small bowl combine 1¼ cups Madeira and currants; let stand one hour.

In a large bowl, cream butter and shortening with sugar until smoothly blended, then thoroughly beat in eggs, one at a time.

Stir together the flour, soda, salt, cinnamon, cloves, and nutmeg.

Drain as much Madeira as possible from currants, adding to it enough more Madeira to make a total of 1¼ cups. Combine the milk with lemon juice and add to Madeira. Alternately add flour mixture and liquid to egg mixture, blending well after each addition. Stir in currants by hand. Pour into a greased, flour-dusted 10-inch tube pan.

Bake in a 375° oven for 1 hour and 15 minutes until center springs back when firmly touched. Cool about 10 minutes and remove from pan. Serve warm or cold, dusted lightly with powdered sugar. Slice in thick or thin pieces as you like. Makes 12 to 20 slices.

Sherry Nut Cake with Lemon Frosting

In order to make the texture of this cake velvet-smooth, grind the almonds into the smallest possible grains. Smooth on the frosting very gently because the cake is fragile.

½ cup (¼ lb.) butter
1 cup sugar
3 egg yolks
½ teaspoon grated lemon peel
1½ cups sifted cake flour
2½ teaspoons baking powder
¼ teaspoon salt
¾ cup finely chopped blanched almonds
¼ cup *each* **dry** or **medium Sherry** and milk
2 egg whites
Lemon frosting (directions follow)

In a large mixing bowl cream butter; gradually add sugar, creaming until sugar is dissolved. Beat in egg yolks with lemon peel until thick and light colored. In a small mixing bowl resift cake flour with baking powder, salt, and stir in nuts. Combine Sherry with the milk. Add to the creamed mixture alternately with dry ingredients beginning and ending with dry ingredients. Beat egg whites until stiff, but not dry. Fold into batter. Pour into a greased 8 or 9-inch spring form pan or a cheesecake pan with removable bottom. Bake in a 350° oven for 45 minutes or until toothpick inserted in the center comes out clean. Allow to cool; remove from pan. Spread with lemon frosting. Makes 12 servings.

Lemon Frosting:

¼ cup soft butter
2 cups sifted powdered sugar
3 tablespoons lemon juice

Cream butter with 1 cup of the powdered sugar; add lemon juice and remaining 1 cup powdered sugar; beat until creamy. Spread on cooled Sherry Nut Cake.

Cookie Balls

These Sherry balls are best when they've "aged" at least a week in the refrigerator. Roll them in coconut, powdered sugar, or colored sugars, and group them in containers.

3 cups vanilla wafer crumbs (2 packages, 4¾ oz. *each*, crushed)
1 cup chopped nuts (pecans, pistachios, or walnuts)
⅓ cup *each* honey and **dry** or **medium Sherry**
Shredded coconut, colored sugars, chopped nuts, or sifted powdered sugar for decoration

In a large bowl, combine the crushed wafer crumbs, nuts, honey, and Sherry. Mix until well blended. Chill overnight. Shape into tiny balls (½ to ¾-inch diameter) and roll in the coconut, colored sugar, chopped nuts, or powdered sugar. Makes about 75 balls.

Fig Trifle

½ pound (8 oz.) sponge cake, cut in 8 slices
½ cup **dry** or **medium Sherry**
8 fresh figs, peeled and sliced
Custard sauce (recipe follows)
½ cup whipping cream
Sugar
3 drops almond extract
2 tablespoons finely chopped nuts

Line a serving bowl with cake slices, sprinkle with Sherry, and cover with sliced figs. Pour cooled custard sauce over fruit; chill at least 6 hours. Top with whipped cream sweetened to taste and flavored with almond extract, then garnish with nut meats. Makes 6 servings.

Custard Sauce:

2 egg yolks, beaten
2 tablespoons sugar
1 cup milk, scalded
2 tablespoons **Sherry**

Beat egg yolks with the sugar and add a little of the hot milk. Combine with remaining milk and cook over hot water (not boiling), stirring occasionally, until mixture coats a metal spoon in an even layer. Cool and flavor with the Sherry. Pour over fruit.

Viennese Fruit Cake

Wines and other liqueurs play a crucial role in the mellowing and aging of fruit cakes.

2 cups (1 lb.) butter or margarine
3⅓ cups sugar
9 eggs, separated
6½ cups all-purpose flour, sifted
2 teaspoons baking powder
1 teaspoon salt
½ teaspoon *each* ground nutmeg and cloves
2 cups *each* **Sherry** and applesauce
3 packages (15 oz. *each*) raisins
About 1 pound mixed candied fruits
2 cups chopped walnuts

Cream butter until fluffy; gradually beat in sugar. Mix in egg yolks until blended. Sift flour again with baking powder, salt, nutmeg, cloves; set aside ½ cup. Add flour mixture alternately with Sherry to creamed mixture. Stir in applesauce. Dredge raisins, candied fruits, and nuts with reserved ½ cup flour; stir fruits and flour into batter. Beat egg whites until they hold firm, moist peaks; fold into batter. Pour an equal portion of the batter into each of 6 loaf pans (5 by 9-inch or 4 by 13-inch) that have been buttered, lined with brown paper, and buttered again. Bake in a 300° oven for 2 hours, or until a wooden skewer inserted into center of cakes comes out clean. If all are baked in one oven, alternate positions on highest and lowest rack half way through baking. Cool on rack, remove from pans. Makes 6 cakes.

CHEERS!

Wine Cocktails, Punches, Hot Beverages

Wine is first a beverage, but many other beverages are complemented by its addition.

A serving size portion for the punches and cocktails given is ½ cup; however, expect guests to have more than one serving. The recipes are scaled to serve just a few as well as group-size servings.

Four hot punches are proposed as fitting for a winter scene served around a crackling fire. One type is actually a soup to sip; since it cooks, the alcohol is lost. The other three are only heated in order to retain the alcohol and full body of the wine.

Chilean Sangría

Sangria is a very popular drink in South American countries. This rendition from Chile combines fresh strawberries and red wine. Use a wine such as a Burgundy or a Zinfandel.

1 cup thinly sliced strawberries (reserve 4 or 5 whole)
½ cup sugar
1 whole lemon, thinly sliced (reserve 1 or 2 slices for garnish)
1 bottle (⅘ qt.) **dry red wine**
2 cups sparkling water, chilled

In a large bowl combine the thinly sliced strawberries, sugar, and lemon slices. Stir mixture with a spoon to bruise the fruit slightly. Pour in the wine, cover and chill at least 1 hour or as long as overnight. Pour mixture through a wire strainer and discard fruit.

In a serving bowl or pitcher, blend the flavored wine with the sparkling water. Drop in the reserved whole strawberries and lemon slices. Add ice to individual glasses, if desired. Makes about 5½ cups, or 11 servings of ½ cup each.

Vermouth Cocktail

Complement your appetizer course with this light cocktail based on Vermouth.

⅛ teaspoon aromatic bitters
1 bottle (⅘ qt.) **sweet Vermouth,** chilled
1½ to 2 quarts club soda, chilled
Lemon peel twists (optional)

Mix in a serving pitcher the bitters, Vermouth, and soda. Serve it immediately in small glasses over ice, with lemon peel if desired. Makes 18 to 24 servings, ½ cup size.

Lemon Champagne Punch

1 can (6 oz.) frozen lemonade concentrate, thawed
Water
2 tablespoons honey
¼ cup curaçao or other orange-flavored liqueur (or undiluted orange juice concentrate, thawed)
1 bottle (⅘ qt.) **Champagne,** chilled

Several hours or the night before serving, measure ½ cup thawed lemonade concentrate (reserving remainder) and mix with 1½ cups water; pour into freezer tray and freeze into ice cubes.

To make punch, blend in a 2-quart or larger pitcher the honey and curaçao. Then add reserved lemonade concentrate and 3/4 cup water. Add the prepared lemonade ice cubes; then carefully pour in the Champagne and mix together. Makes about 10 servings. 1/2 cup size.

Muscat Wine Punch

3 bottles (4/5 qt. *each*) **Riesling,** chilled
1 bottle (4/5 qt.) **Black Muscat,** chilled
2 bottles (1 qt. *each*) sparkling water, chilled
2 cups muscat grapes, washed, stems removed
Ice (optional)

To serve, blend Riesling, Black Muscat, and sparkling water in a punch bowl. Add grapes to the punch. Ladle the punch into wine glasses, adding a few grapes to each serving. Add ice if desired. Makes about 40 servings, 1/2 cup size.

Orange Sherry Cocktail

2 cans (6 oz. *each*) frozen orange juice concentrate
Water
2 cups **dry Sherry**

Prepare orange juice in a pitcher as directed on the can. Stir in the Sherry and chill. Makes 16 servings, 1/2 cup size.

Dried Fruit Cordials

Certain dried fruits, when immersed in white wine fortified with brandy, will give the wine their fruity flavor. The dried fruits take on new character as well. Use a wine such as a Chablis or Chenin Blanc; or, a Rhine or Gewürztraminer.

1 pound dried apricots, prunes without pits, pears, or peaches
1 bottle (4/5 qt.) or 3 1/3 cups **dry white wine**
1 cup **brandy**
2 cups sugar

In a glass, ceramic, or stainless steel container combine dried fruit with wine, brandy, and sugar, stirring well. Cover tightly and set aside at room temperature for at least a week to allow flavors to develop. Stir occasionally for the first few days until the sugar is dissolved.

After one week all fruits but the peaches will have the texture of poached fruit and are ready to eat; peaches will be firmer. The fruit taste in the wine reaches its maximum intensity in three or four weeks. After about six weeks the fruit may become softer than desired and should be removed; the wine keeps indefinitely.

To serve, offer a piece of fruit in a glass of wine or serve alone. Makes about 1 1/2 quarts or 18 servings of 1/3 cup size.

Sparkling Pink Punch

Bright pink rhubarb and strawberries give this punch its color; it makes enough to serve a large party. Use a wine such as a Chablis or a Chenin Blanc, along with the Champagne.

10 pounds rhubarb
5 pounds sugar
1 tablespoon *each* grated orange and lemon peel
1 teaspoon salt
1 1/2 quarts (6 cups) water
3 to 4 quarts hulled fresh strawberries (or about 6 packages frozen whole strawberries, 10 oz. *each*)
1 large can (46 oz.) pineapple juice
2 cups lemon juice
10 to 15 pounds ice, cubes or a block
2 or 3 bottles (4/5 quart *each*) **Champagne,** chilled
2 bottles (4/5 quart *each*) **dry white wine,** chilled

Wash rhubarb, cut into small pieces, and combine in a large kettle with the sugar, orange and lemon peel, salt, and water. Bring to a boil and cook until rhubarb is tender (about 10 minutes); let cool. Whirl, a portion at a time, until smooth in an electric blender (or force through a food mill); this much can be done ahead and chilled.

Hull and purée or crush the berries, add to rhubarb base with pineapple and lemon juice. Pour over ice in a large punch bowl and let stand until cold; stir occasionally. To serve, add the chilled champagne and white wine. Makes about 4 gallons or 128 servings, 1/2 cup size.

Wine Syllabub

This punch with a frothy top is a near-cousin to eggnog, but with fewer calories and a light taste of wine and lemon. Use a wine such as a Chablis or a Pinot Blanc.

- 1 cup sugar
- 1 bottle (⅘ qt.) **dry white wine**
- 3 tablespoons grated lemon peel
- ⅓ cup lemon juice
- 3 cups cold milk
- 2 cups (1 pt.) half-and-half
- 4 egg whites
- Sprinkling of nutmeg

Combine ½ cup of the sugar with the wine, lemon peel, and lemon juice in mixing bowl. Stir until the sugar is completely dissolved; chill well. In a punch bowl, blend in the milk and half-and-half. Pour in the wine mixture and beat with a rotary beater or wire whip until frothy. Beat the egg whites until stiff peaks form; gradually add the remaining ½ cup sugar, beating until stiff glossy peaks form. Float spoonful puffs of this meringue on top of the punch. Sprinkle them lightly with nutmeg. Makes about 18 servings, ½ cup size.

White Wine Fruit Punch

Allow some of the fruits and spices to stand together for a day to mingle flavors. Use a wine such as a dry Sauterne or a dry Semillon.

- 1 medium-sized pineapple, peeled and cut into chunks
- ½ cup firmly packed brown sugar
- ½ whole nutmeg, grated (or 1 teaspoon ground nutmeg)
- 1 vanilla bean, slit in half lengthwise
- 2 *each* grapefruit and oranges, peeled and sectioned
- Peel of 1 lime, pared with a vegetable peeler
- Juice of 2 limes (about ¼ cup)
- 1 bottle (⅘ qt.) **dry white wine,** chilled
- 6 cups fruit juice (orange, pineapple, grapefruit, or a combination)

Place in a large bowl or pitcher the pineapple, brown sugar, nutmeg, and vanilla bean. Mix and cover. Chill for 12 to 24 hours. Add grapefruit and orange sections. Twist strips of lime peel to release oils and drop in with fruit. Add lime juice, wine, and fruit juice. Pour over ice in a large punch bowl. Makes about 2½ quarts, or 20 servings of ½ cup size.

Champagne Orange Cocktail

- 1 bottle (⅘ quart) **Champagne,** chilled
- 4 cups chilled orange juice

In a chilled pitcher or punch bowl combine the Champagne and orange juice just before ready to serve. Add ice cubes if desired. Makes about 14 servings, ½ cup size.

Port Wine Punch

Full-bodied Port wine makes the base of this punch; cranberry juice cocktail adds fruit flavor and rosy glow.

- 1 quart bottle ginger ale
- ¾ cup cranberry juice cocktail, chilled
- 1 bottle (⅘ qt.) **Port**, chilled

Several hours or the night before serving, freeze half of the bottle of ginger ale into cubes; recap bottle tightly. To make punch, mix together in a 2½-quart pitcher the chilled cranberry juice cocktail and chilled Port wine. Add prepared ice cubes; stir in remaining 2 cups ginger ale. Makes about 15 servings, ½ cup size.

Julglögg (Christmas Wine)

Make the first part of this zesty Scandinavian glögg (pronounced *glug*) at least 2 days before you plan to serve it. Use a wine combination of a dry Sauterne or a Sauvignon Blanc *and* a Burgundy or a Gamay.

10 whole cardamom pods, broken open
5 whole cloves
1 stick cinnamon (3 to 4 inches long)
1 cup *each* whole blanched almonds and raisins
4 dried figs
Peel from 3 oranges cut in long strips with a vegetable peeler
2 bottles (⅘ qt. *each*) **dry white wine**
1 bottle (⅘ qt.) **dry red wine**
½ cup sugar

In a large saucepan combine the cardamom, cloves, cinnamon, almonds, raisins, figs, and orange peel strips and one of the bottles of white wine. Cover and heat quickly until hot to touch; take care not to boil. Cool, cover, and store until time to serve—at least 2 days.

Before serving, remove the figs, orange peel, and spices, leaving raisins and almonds in the wine. Add the remaining bottle of white wine and the bottle of red wine along with the sugar; heat to sipping temperature; *do not boil.* Serve hot with some of the raisins and almonds in each cup. Makes 20 servings, ½ cup size.

Hot Cider Punch

This hot spicy punch goes well before winter holiday dinners or after skiing. Use a wine such as a Sauterne or dry Sherry.

3 quarts cider or apple juice
2 to 3 bottles (⅘ qt. *each*) **white wine** or **dry Sherry**
12 whole cloves
4 cinnamon sticks (*each* 3 to 4 inches long)
Orange slices (unpeeled)

Mix cider, wine, cloves, and cinnamon sticks in a large kettle; let sit at least 30 minutes. Heat just until hot immediately before serving. Garnish with orange slices. Makes about 35 to 45 servings, ½ cup size.

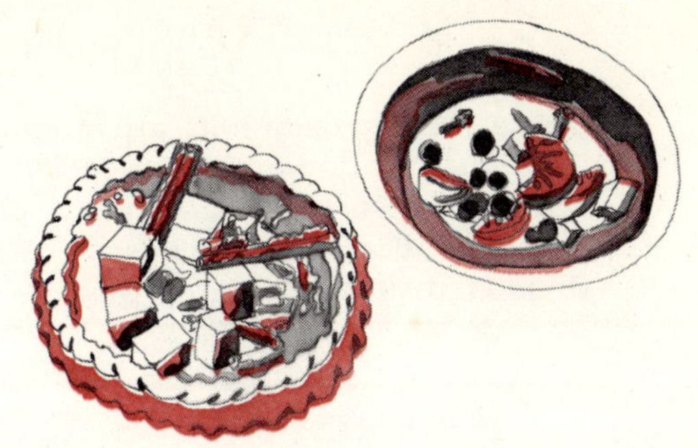

Hot Tomato Juice Cocktail

Use a wine such as a Rhine or a Riesling.

3 cups tomato juice
3 whole cloves
1 tablespoon lemon juice
1½ teaspoons *each* sugar and salt
Dash of pepper
¾ cup **dry white wine**

Combine tomato juice, cloves, lemon juice, sugar, salt, and pepper in a saucepan and bring to simmering. Remove from heat and stir in wine. Serve hot. Makes 6 servings, ½ cup size.

White Wine Sipping Soup

This "soup" is flexible enough to be served as a before or after dinner drink as an alternate for hot buttered rum or spiced wine. Use a wine such as a Rhine or a Sylvaner.

1 tablespoon butter or margarine
1 tablespoon all-purpose flour
1 bottle (⅘ quart) **white wine**
1 stick cinnamon (3 or 4 inches long)
Peel of 1 lemon, pared in thin strips (with a vegetable peeler)
3 tablespoons sugar
3 egg yolks
Toasted croutons

In a 1½ to 2-quart saucepan, melt the butter and blend in flour; cook slowly for 2 minutes. Gradually stir in the wine; add the cinnamon stick, lemon peel, and sugar. Simmer for 5 minutes. Beat the egg yolks until thick, blend in some of the hot soup, then stir egg mixture back into soup. Remove from heat, take out cinnamon, pour soup into a preheated soup tureen or ladle immediately into mugs. Top each with a few toasted croutons, if desired. Makes about 6 servings, ½ cup size.

WINE COOKERY CHART

These recommendations are intended as suggestions, not hard-and-fast rules. This qualification applies especially to the column on amounts of wine to use. Many experienced cooks add wine entirely by taste, just as they do salt. Use these amounts as rough estimates, to be made more precise when you flavor each individual dish. To select a red or white table wine, see choices on pages 8-9.

	FOODS	AMOUNT	WINES
Soups	Cream soups	1 or 2 teaspoons per serving	Dry white wine or Sherry
	Meat and vegetable soups	1 or 2 teaspoons per serving	Dry white or red wine or Sherry
	Bouillon or clear soups	1 or 2 teaspoons per serving	Dry white or red wine, Sherry, or dry Vermouth
Sea-foods	Fish and shellfish	½ cup per pound	Dry white wine
Poultry and Game	Chicken, broiled (for basting) or sautéed	¼ cup per pound	Dry white or red wine
	Braised chicken	¼ cup per pound	Dry white wine
	Gravy for chicken and turkey	2 tablespoons per cup	Dry white or red wine, Sherry or dry Vermouth
	Rabbit, braised	¼ cup per pound	Dry white or red wine
	Duck (wild or domestic), roast (for basting)	¼ cup per pound	Dry red wine
	Venison, roast (for basting), pot roast, or stew	¼ cup per pound	Dry red wine
	Pheasant, roast (for basting) or sauté	¼ cup per pound	Dry white or red wine or Sherry
Meats	Beef roast, pot roast, or stew	¼ cup per pound	Dry red wine
	Lamb and veal, roast or stew	¼ cup per pound	Dry white wine or Rosé
	Pork, roast (for basting)	¼ cup per pound	Dry red or white wine, Rosé or Sherry
	Gravy for roasts	2 tablespoons per cup	Dry red or white wine or Sherry
	Ham (whole), baked (for basting)	2 cups	Port, Muscatel, or Rosé
	Liver, braised	¼ cup per pound	Dry red or white wine
	Kidneys, braised	¼ cup per pound	Sherry or red wine
	Tongue, boiled	½ cup per pound	Dry red wine
	Sweetbreads	¼ cup per pound	Dry white wine or dry Vermouth
Cheese Dishes	Soufflés and other lightly flavored dishes	½ to 1 cup per pound of cheese	Dry white wine
	Robust-flavored cheese dishes	½ to 1 cup per pound of cheese	Dry white or red wine
Egg Dishes	Scrambled, omelets, baked	1 teaspoon to 1 tablespoon per egg	Dry white wine or dry Vermouth
Sauces	Cream sauce and variations	1 tablespoon per cup	Sherry, dry Vermouth, or white wine
	Brown sauce and variations	1 tablespoon per cup	Sherry or red wine
	Tomato sauce	1 tablespoon per cup	Sherry or dry red wine
	Cheese sauce	1 tablespoon per cup	Sherry or dry white wine
	Dessert sauces	1 tablespoon per cup	Port, Muscatel, sweet Sherry, or sweet white wine
Casse-roles	Meat, poultry, seafood, egg, cheese	1 tablespoon per cup of sauce	Use wine suggested for protein ingredient
Fruits	Compotes and fruit cups	2 tablespoons per serving	Port, Muscatel, Sherry, Champagne, or sweet white wine
Desserts	Puddings, refrigerator desserts	1 tablespoon per serving	Any dessert wine, sweet white wine, or sweet Champagne

Index